TOWARD A THEOLOGY OF HISTORY

Toward a Theology of History

By

J. V. LANGMEAD CASSERLEY

HOLT, RINEHART AND WINSTON

NEW YORK   CHICAGO   SAN FRANCISCO

Published simultaneously in Canada by
HOLT, RINEHART AND WINSTON OF CANADA, LIMITED

First Edition

Library of Congress Catalog Card Number: 65–10130

81326–0115

PRINTED IN GREAT BRITAIN

FOR PAUL AND GRET,
WITH MUCH LOVE

PREFACE

THIS book is concerned with theology of history rather than philosophy of history. It is conceived and written from within the traditions of Christian thought but, as so often, the problems themselves have been observed and defined outside the traditions of Christian thought. Thus we should not distinguish too sharply between the theology of something or other and the philosophy of the same thing. The problem for the theologian is the same as the problem for the philosopher, and it is probably true that in most cases it is the philosopher who draws the theologian's attention to the problem. The theologian, who must also be something of a philosopher, studies what the philosophers have had to say about the particular problem, finds it unsatisfactory even from a philosophical point of view—of course, for philosophical reasons—and then proceeds to inquire whether his own theological concepts can interpret more profoundly and clarify understanding in a way and to an extent to which merely or purely philosophical methods and concepts have failed to do. Thus the theologian thinks and writes theologically about problems which have already received more or less adequate philosophical definition, and it must therefore be difficult to decide upon any precise point at which for him philosophy ends and theology begins. Perhaps there is no such point, and the kind of thing to be found in a book like this should be described either as philosophical theology or theological philosophy. But whatever the name by which we entitle it, the thing itself remains the same kind of thing, the theologically inspired and guided meditations of a Christian philosopher. The reader who does not like or want that kind of thing had better read no further.

In this book I have begun with the biblical idea of revelation, taking it to be the point within theology at which the problems examined by the philosopher of history are clearly seen to arise just as insistently for the theologian. From there we shall branch out into a critique of modern and contemporary historical methodology, and into somewhat preliminary inquiries into the epistemology and ontology of history. At the end of the book, since the philosophy of history is never far from the activity of prophecy, is indeed its intellectual counterpart and interpreter, we turn to the contemporary situation and try to apprehend to-day's answer to the question pressed upon Jeremiah by the distraught Zedekiah: 'Is there any word from the Lord?'

This book is based upon a series of *Gates Lectures* given at Grinnell College, Iowa, during the fall of 1960. Since then I have added new material and revised the text here and there, but at least three-quarters of what is contained in this volume was originally written to be heard rather than read, which may account somewhat for its form and style. I am extremely grateful to the faculty and students of Grinnell College for the graciousness with which I was received, and the enthusiasm with which my lectures were attended. To have been selected as Gates Lecturer is a great honour, and I am glad to be able to offer this book as a testimony to the value of the stimulus and opportunity which the invitation to give lectures of this kind presents to visiting teachers like me, who might otherwise too easily 'run to seed' in the ordinary performance of their accustomed duties.

J. V. LANGMEAD CASSERLEY

CONTENTS

TOWARD A THEOLOGY OF HISTORY

Chapter I

THE CONCEPT OF REVELATION

REVELATION is the basic intellectual category of religious thought. Revelation distinguishes religion from mere religiosity and theology from philosophy. Religiosity is a human activity, a distinctive kind of human initiative, whereas religion is a human response. Religious philosophy is a speculative intellectual activity closely allied to religiosity, whereas theology is a form of thought in some ways more akin to science than to speculative philosophy, in which the thinker is disciplined and constrained by the character of his datum, a certain body of given experience to the interpretation of which he must devote all his labours and to the authority of which he must ultimately defer. Thus we may say that the intellectual character and quality of a system of religious doctrine is very largely determined by the concept of revelation which it presupposes.

Of course, it is possible to have a system of religious thought and teaching without any doctrine of revelation at all, and indeed in non-theistic religions like Hinayana Buddhism this is what happens. Revelation is inconceivable apart from the idea of an active personal God who takes the initiative and reveals himself. In Hinayana Buddhism, Buddha sits under the fig tree and in a classic moment of piercing insight perceives the truth about human existence. This is not revelation, because no god reveals himself; Buddha's vision is attributed to his genius; when he expounds it to others, this also is not revelation but simply one wise and holy man declaring to his fellows the content of his wisdom. Of course, at a later date, in Mahayana Buddhism, Buddha became a kind of incarnation of the godhead, or the prime example of a whole series of such incarnations, so that his insight was interpreted as a supernaturally conditioned one. We may say that Mahayana Buddhism has a doctrine of revelation, because in its concept of the eternal buddha-spirit it has become at least quasi-theistic, whereas the Hinayana Buddhism, which is almost certainly closer to the original Buddhism of Buddha himself, has no doctrine of revelation.

More generally, we may say that wherever, to use Julian Huxley's phrase, we have 'religion without revelation,' religion redounds not to the glory of God but to the glory of man. Man is conceived as a spiritual animal with a yearning for ultimate truth—and this, after all, is sometimes, although by no means always, the case—and his religious consciousness or experience is that which satisfies his yearning more fully and profoundly. In so far as we are in touch with any kind of religious truth, it is human religious genius that seeks it out and lays it bare. This differs from some types of philosophy, for example, the more vulgar kinds of empiricism, by holding that truth is to be found in the depths rather than on the surface of things; but there are many other kinds of philosophy which would agree. I have chosen to call this religiosity rather than religion, and we may say that for religiosity man is the active religious agent, the seeker who finds, whereas in genuine religion it is God who seeks and finds and man who is found.

But even if we ignore mere religiosity, with its concept of religion without revelation, we can still, even within the area of revealed religion, even within Christian thought itself, find two very different ways of defining and understanding the process of revelation. According to one doctrine, revelation is to be found in the inspiration of holy men, by a self-revealing process which takes place in the heart of their spirituality. Holy men are so inspired by God that they deliver to their fellows infallible oracles. Thus, for example, we meet with oracles in classical paganism. Even within the Bible God inspires the prophets to speak his word, or gives the Law to Moses on the holy mount. Similarly in Islam the Archangel Gabriel dictates the Koran to Mohammed in the cave, and at a much later date an essentially Korannic conception of the writing of the Scriptures began to gain ground within Christendom. The result of this assimilation of our concept of the way in which the scriptures were composed to the Koran's teaching about the method of its own composition is nowadays called fundamentalism, for which, in effect, the Bible is the Christian Koran, although more frequently we describe the Koran as the Moslem Bible.

Of course, fundamentalists are often very good Christian people, and it is possible to interpret the contemporary fundamentalist revival as a genuine movement of protest against something which ought to be protested against, but we must add that the protest is made unfortunately in a manner which cannot be sustained and defended. All fundamentalism imports into Christianity and the Christian interpretation of the scriptures attitudes which are foreign to both Christianity and the Bible, and which, as a matter of historical fact, Christians learned and derived from Islam rather than from Christianity. Nowadays the Christian West is so much more advanced in the ways of civilization and the arts of technology than the Moslem lands of the Middle East that we often forget that during the Middle Ages, not so many centuries ago, the situation was the other way round, and the intellectualism then starting once more in the West was profoundly influenced by the brilliant triumphs of Moslem forms of civilization. The extent of Arabic influence on mathematics and the growth of the sciences is well known, but that it was equally great, if not even greater, in philosophy and theology is sometimes ignored. The fact remains, however, that from the twelfth century onwards almost down to our own day the Bible was regarded as a collection of inspired and infallible oracles *dictated*, as Pope Leo XIII said, by the Holy Spirit. So much so that many, perhaps most, people now regard this as the traditional Christian view, and some even equate it with orthodoxy.

A more careful examination, however, has convinced many modern theologians that this is very far from being the case, that oracular notions involving some kind of dictation of the scriptures by the Holy Spirit are not merely external to the Biblical and Christian tradition, but actually alien to it. It is certainly true that in the Old Testament the Lord revealed his word to the prophets and that they were accustomed to prelude their messages to the people with the solemn words: 'Thus saith the Lord God.' But when we examine the context of the divine message it normally turns out to be some kind of interpretation of historical episodes—in which the Hebrew nation is either richly blessed or, more frequently, struck by catastrophe—in terms of the will, the judgement and the purpose of God, so that God himself is revealed not primarily in the word given to the prophet but in the event which the prophetic word interprets. Similarly in the New Testament epistles, for example those of St. Paul, the revelation is not primarily in the Apostolic formulae, but in the actual occurrence of the birth, sacrificial ministry, death and resurrection of Jesus Christ, the Son of God. The shape of the two testaments precisely corresponds: first the testimony to the event, in the one case the history of Israel, in the other the life of Jesus, and then the inspired interpretation, always with the revelation in the events rather than in the interpretation, the function of the interpretation being to make it clear that

4

the revelation is given in the events. Thus the role of the epistles and apostolic writings in the New Testament corresponds to that of prophets in the Old Testament, and the Gospels occupy the same place in the New Testament as the historical records of Israel play in the Old.

This has led many contemporary theologians to the view that in Christianity there are no revealed doctrines at all, but only the great revealing acts of God, which the Christian doctrines interpret and comprehend with at least partial success. Revelation, we are told by these theologians, is given in history, not in propositions, and we even find the phrase 'non-propositional revelation' widely current.

Now to speak of non-propositional revelation seems to me to raise a question which in fact need not be raised at all in order to state the truth which underlies the contemporary rejection of any oracular concepts of revelation. Of course, wherever meaning is communicated, propositions which report and define it arise in the human mind. To perceive a meaning is to utter a proposition, even if only to oneself. If revelation involves perceiving the meaning of events it clearly involves propositions. If there is any primitive stage in the communication in which we have mere events without propositions, it is a merely conjectured stage in which revelation is held to be revelation before it has in fact revealed anything, raising the ghosts of old philosophical conundrums like, 'What is experience before anyone has experienced it?' which have led us into so many difficulties in the past. Clearly revelation is a process which includes not only events but also the power and capacity of the events to evoke in responsive minds the propositions which interpret and report their meaning. Thus we cannot possibly consent to any definition of this process which includes the term 'non-propositional.' Non-oracular would be a better term, and one which would after all get equally well at the underlying truth which people who talk about non-propositional revelation are seeking to express. Revelation is given in events not in oracles, in acts of God rather than in religious doctrines.

We must also add that even if we wish to avoid any notion of the Holy Spirit dictating oracles to human recipients and intermediaries, we must not for that reason exclude the Holy Spirit entirely from the process in which the propositions are framed and the doctrines laid down. On the contrary, the area of human response to revelation, the experience in which men perceive that there is revelation and gradually build up a more and more adequate interpretation of it, is essentially the area in which the Holy Spirit is active. If we ought not to say that the Holy Spirit dictated the propositions or the doctrines, we must nevertheless insist that the Holy Spirit is really behind the propositions and the doctrines, and that they come to us through the Church laden with His authority. In other words, we must not interpret this new insight into the meaning of revelation as a new, latter-day sanction for the hoary old error which marks out a strict dichotomony between the world of the revealing Bible and the work of the interpreting Church. On the contrary, the work of the interpreting Church, guided and empowered by the Holy Spirit, begins and can be traced within the Bible itself. Thus the work of the interpreting Church has a biblical sanction because it has a biblical beginning. What the Bible incorporates cannot, in the name of the Bible, be rejected, and what the Bible begins must for any truly biblical piety be zealously continued. As the Church without the Bible lacks foundations, so the Bible without the Church lacks the visible evidences of vitality and growth.

Perhaps one of the most balanced statements of this contemporary view of revelation is to be found in chapter twelve of William Temple's Gifford Lectures, *Nature, God*

6

and Man.[1] Dr. Temple begins by laying down clearly the biblical principle that revelation is in events: 'Plainly it (i.e. revelation) could not be in the book unless it is first in the events. And this is the witness of the book itself; for the prophets ... were largely occupied in reading the lessons of history to the people whose history it was.'[2] Yet Dr. Temple did not make the mistake of supposing that the revelation is 'merely' in the events. In his view, if the biblical event itself is rooted in the divine transcendence, our appreciation of its meaning is rooted in the divine immanence. He who reveals himself to us publicly and dramatically in some particular event, or course of events, is also the God whose wisdom guides and overshadows us, secretly and often without recognition, throughout the whole course of our creaturely life. The principle of revelation, Dr. Temple tells us, is 'the coincidence of event and interpretation,'[3] and he adds in a footnote that 'the appreciation need not be contemporaneous with the event. But till it comes the event, through revelatory in its own character, is not yet fully revelation. If no one had recognized Christ, the Incarnation would have occurred, but it would have failed to effect a revelation of God.'[4] Thus the divine authority lurks concealed within the propositions and doctrines which interpret the event, just as truly as the Divine majesty is only implicit in the event itself until the event has evoked the propositions and doctrines which make it explicit. It seems clear that we cannot use a doctrine of this kind to drive a new wedge between the revealing Bible and the interpreting Church. The God who reveals himself in the events of history is at the same time the God who reveals himself in the prophetic interpretation of the historic events.

Nor must we make the mistake of supposing that if the Bible is a human record of the acts of God, all that is

---

[1] The Gifford Lectures for 1932–3 and 1933–4. Macmillan, London, 1934.
[2] Op. cit., pp. 308.   [3] Ibid., p. 315.   [4] Ibid., p. 315 (n.).

thereby revealed is simply that the acts of God are the acts of God. If I observe that a certain man constantly performs kind actions, what is revealed to me is not merely that on certain specific and ascertainable occasions this particular man has acted in a kindly and considerate manner, but rather that he is all the time a kind and considerate man, even upon occasions which do not evoke or receive his kindly consideration. After all, kindness and consideration do not make up a complete human character, and such a man may also be courageous and honest and have many other admirable characteristics which will be revealed equally vividly on other occasions and by other acts. In other words, the biblically recorded acts of God really reveal God, and our interpretation of them passes beyond the mere repetition of our testimony to the occurrence of the divine acts into more profound statements about the divine justice, the divine purpose and the divine love. Or, to put it in another way, the process of the divine revelation is, of course, temporal and in history, but the content of the divine revelation, the *revelatum*, is eternal and transcends all history. God does this or that in time, but he *is* in eternity, and what he reveals in time is precisely what he is in eternity.

I say this in order to make it clear that this particular way of stating the Christian doctrine of revelation is anything but a peculiar characteristic of that particular brand of theological teaching which is known as protestant neo-orthodoxy. Of course, it is true that most of the so-called neo-orthodox theologians insist strongly on this new formulation of the doctrine of revelation, often perhaps too stridently and without the sanity and balance characteristic of Dr. Temple. They often tend to do so in a manner which divides the biblical revelation too sharply from the work of the interpreting Church. They detect the presence of the Living God in the biblical events, but not always the influence of the Holy Spirit upon the

8

formation of the theological tradition, with the curious result that the so-called 'neo-orthodoxy' is often far less orthodox than to many of us seems desirable.

Again, some writers of this kind lean towards brands of semi-positivistic philosophy according to which all we can know about an active being is simply that he has performed certain acts. For such brands of philosophy man is simply a kind of general class name for the series of human acts, and God is a similar name for the series of divine acts. We have had serious philosophical movements in this century which have attempted to substitute the notion of process or function for the notion of being. Man, from such a point of view, is simply the name of the human process, God simply the name of the divine, creative process. Now, of course, it is one thing to say that on the whole the great classical philosophers were more impressed by the idea of space than by the idea of time, and that because we *are* in space and act in time they therefore gave more weight to the notion of sheer being than to the notion of activity. This observation has a certain amount of rather limited truth, but such a situation can hardly be remedied by a sharp reaction which gives more weight to the notion of time than to the notion of space, and sometimes threatens to reduce itself to the absurdity of holding that reality consists of an enormous number of active processes with no-one or nothing to perform them.

Whatever may be the weaknesses of the so-called process philosophy, it has certainly attracted a considerable number of thinkers who are apt to give great weight to history and the Bible. Sometimes we are even told that this process philosophy precisely fits the biblical idea of a living, active God, a philosophical judgement which is in my view very questionable indeed. Biblically speaking, we must always remember that the God who reveals himself is also the God who hides himself. Revelation means that indeed we know God, but it never means that

9

we know all of God. God may be a known and revealed mystery, but he nevertheless remains a mystery. A mystery is not something which it is impossible to know or of which it is impossible to make any sense. A mystery is simply that which we cannot get to the bottom of. It is the bottomlessness of reality which compels us to acknowledge that wherever we are intellectually active and concerned we are always and necessarily surrounded by mystery. Our knowledge is always transcended by the reality that it knows. To put it another way, the divine being reveals himself through the divine acts, but the divine being nevertheless transcends the divine acts, and this truth is essential to any adequate grasp of the nature of biblical revelation. This is why any full response of man to God requires love as well as knowledge. Knowledge only knows what it knows, but love grasps both what is known and what is unknown in their intrinsic unity and integrity; because it loves what it knows, it goes on to love even what it does not know. This is a truth as essential to human relations, like friendship and marriage, as to the religious condition, and we shall have occasion to return to it at a later stage.

Philosophically speaking, the process philosophy fails because it cannot see that potentiality is just as significant a feature of real life and history as actuality. A particular man is never merely the being who has performed certain acts. He is also the being who has not performed many other acts which he might equally well have performed. He has not merely succeeded in becoming this, he has also failed to become that, or perhaps deliberately chosen not to become it. A life, in other words, is not merely a thing of positive actuality, but also of latent potentialities, unused capacities, unrealized opportunities. A man is never merely the class of his acts, he is also the source and cause of his inaction. He is a not-doing as much as a doing, and this because he is a being rather than a process. The category of being still remains more fundamental than the category of process, indeed, it remains fundamental even to the understanding of process, for process is a continuity, not merely a series of discrete acts, rendered staccato.

In general, then, we may endorse the view that biblical revelation is given us in events rather than in oracles dictated to the human mind by some kind of supernatural agency. In embracing this doctrine, however, we must be careful not to drive a wedge between the revealing events and the receiving, interpreting, appropriating Church, and perhaps even more careful not to formulate this concept of revelation in such a way as to tie this new truth to a very defective, visibly declining and shortly no doubt to be altogether defunct, type of ephemeral philosophy particularly characteristic of the first half of the twentieth century. To put it in other words, the doctrine that biblical revelation is given primarily in events need not be identified with either neo-orthodox theology on the one hand or with Whiteheadian, process philosophy on the other![1]

Having made these careful *caveats* I should like to say that in my view this concept of revelation, as defined in Dr. Temple's finest contribution to philosophical theology, would seem to me to be inescapably true. This is not merely our concept of biblical revelation in the twentieth century, it is, in fact, the Bible's own concept of revelation. God acts in the history of Israel and in the life of Christ. Men perceive not merely that these events are, they also perceive what these events mean, and in the acting and the perception is to be found the revelation. God himself is as active in the human perception as he is in the events which are perceived. Just as in the events themselves God acts through the human, so in the human perception and interpretation God is also active. From the point of view

[1] See Appendix to Chapter 1, p. 29.

of the merely gross factualist there would appear to be no active agent in the entire drama apart from men. For Christ can be interpreted, with at least *prima facie* plausibility, as a mere man and Israel as a mere nation, just as the story of the growth of Christian institutions, experience and doctrine can be interpreted as mere history or mere sociology, but in such a case the meaning of the event is hidden from our eyes. The important thing is to see the activity of God on both sides of the line, both in what we perceive and in the way in which we perceive it. Revelation, we may say, then, is divinely initiated event plus divinely guided interpretation. The interpretation perceives the meaning of the event and the meaning of the event is the will, the purpose, the justice and the love of Almighty God.

The subject of this book is the relation of this way of conceiving revelation to the philosophy of history, and perhaps at this point we should briefly review the kinds of question with which the philosophy of history is concerned. In the past the philosophy of history has been treated by professional historians with considerable suspicion and reserve. They have felt, and often with good reason, that the philosophy of history has threatened to arrive at historical conclusions without the discipline of historical research and analysis. It is undeniably true that some philosophers of history have attempted to deduce from their own speculative principles what the course of history ought to be or must be like, and then to examine history rather superficially with the partisan purpose of showing that that in fact is just what it is like. The philosopher of history has sometimes deduced his basic conclusions from speculative metaphysics and then, by manipulating the evidences, read his conclusions into them rather than out of them. If this criticism involves a mistaken view of the whole purpose and character of the philosophy of history then it must be agreed that it was the philosophers of history themselves who made the mistake in the first place. Yet in my view it is very plainly a mistake. It is no more the purpose of the philosophy of history to reach and provide any positive conclusions about the course of history, or to dictate to the historian what his conclusions must or ought to be, than it is the purpose of the philosophy of nature and natural science to arrive at positive scientific theories. The philosophy of history properly understood is a reflection upon historical activity, an evaluation of its status, an isolation of its presuppositions, and a deduction of its ultimate implications. The philosophy of history does not draw any conclusions about history considered as a series of events, but it does draw conclusions about history considered as an intellectual and scholarly activity.

In modern academic and intellectual parlance, the word *history* has acquired an ambiguity which did not belong to it in earlier times. Sometimes we use the word *history* to describe a particular form of knowing, researching and discovering, and the particular body of knowledge which emerges out of such an intellectual activity. From this point of view history is what historians do, what they know, think and write about. But at other times we use the word *history* to denote not the particular form and content of historical knowledge, but the datum itself which the historian partly knows and partly does not know. Thus, for example, when a journalist described Sir Winston Churchill as a man who has made history, the probability is that he was not referring to the fact that Sir Winston Churchill wrote books of history but rather to the important, indeed, dominating part, which he played in events that will probably be a major theme of historical examination and exposition so long as our civilization lasts. Thus the one word is used to describe at the same time both our knowing and the objective reality which our knowing knows. Not a few difficulties arise whenever this ambiguity is unobserved. I shall try to preserve the distinction by speaking sometimes of history A (the form and content of our historical knowledge) and sometimes of history B (the actual courses of events located in past time which history A knows or seeks to know). At other times I shall distinguish between historiography (history A in written or stated form) and history, by which I shall mean history B. Whenever the word history is used without the letters A or B, I shall in fact mean history B, and the contrast will be with historiography.

The questions which the philosopher of history has to examine I take to be of three kinds. First, he must consider the problem of historical methodology. How does the historian set about his task? What methodological alternatives lie before him between which he must choose? What do these distinctive methodologies presuppose? What general conclusions do they imply?

Secondly, the philosophy of history must examine the closely-related problem of historical epistemology. What can the historian know? What is the relation between the historical and other forms of knowledge?

Clearly some writers take the view that there are other forms of knowledge which historical knowledge closely resembles. 'History,' said the late Professor Bury, 'is a science; no less and no more.'[1] Obviously this is an epistemological position. Of course, until we know precisely what the speaker means by a science we cannot tell exactly what he means by this assertion; but certainly he means that whatever a science is, no doubt with a few relatively superficial qualifications, our history A is also. Others, of course, would take very different positions, some affiliating history more closely to aesthetic and dramatic forms of activity, others perhaps insisting that

[1] *Selected Essays*, ed. Temperley, Cambridge, 1930, p. 4.

historical knowledge is something *sui generis* which cannot be reduced to any other form of knowledge. Questions of this kind clearly fall within the province of the philosophy of history.

The last, most exacting and perhaps most important, of the inquiries which devolve upon the philosophy of history we may call historical ontology. Whereas the questions which arise in historical methodology and historical epistemology are primarily concerned with what we have called history A, historical ontology is interested almost exclusively in history B. What is the status of historical events in the scale of reality? What is the relationship between that form of changing reality investigated by history A and other kinds of reality or actuality which indeed press hardly upon history but in another sense do not belong to it? For example, as we investigate the long record of historical change we are struck by the fact that all history is environed and pressed upon by certain physical and biological and perhaps psychological constants which remain the same throughout the whole process. The historian sees these as realities which have no history, but which are nevertheless not irrelevant to the course of history. Now it is true that since Darwin's day we have been led more and more to the conclusion that these physical and biological constants are not in fact quite so constant as they seem, and that even they have their own peculiar kind of history. On the other hand, the tempo of that history which we call evolution is extremely slow, and such knowledge of it as we possess is not the kind of knowledge which we describe as historical. The story of the development of the physical universe and the various biological species is indeed analogous to history—sometimes we call it natural history to distinguish it from human history—but it is certainly not history in the usual sense of the word. The tempo of human history is so much more rapid than that of natural history that to all intents and purposes the physical and biological conditions of human history can still be reckoned as constants so far as human history is concerned.

Whether there are any genuine psychological constants is perhaps a little more questionable. Human nature, men say, does not change. *Plus ça change, plus c'est la même chose.* 'The thing that has been, it is that which shall be, and that which is done is that which shall be done, and there is no new thing under the sun.'[1] Such verdicts as these are not so obviously true as have sometimes been supposed, nor perhaps true to quite the extent which has been supposed. Yet nevertheless there is indeed something in them. They require a good deal of qualifications but such dicta cannot be rejected altogether. I remember a BBC performance of a play by Menander reconstructed from Greek fragments by the late Professor Gilbert Murray. It turned out to be an amusing comedy in which two men quarrelled about a woman. One does not have to be a Platonist in order to see that man himself, considered as a kind of concrete universal, is one of the great constants of human history, and that through all the very real changes which he undergoes man, the human reality, remains recognizably man. When history and archaeology enable us to look over enormous gaps of time, what we are looking at by these means, even if we are looking at cave men who painted their stony walls, are recognizably human beings akin to ourselves, very different from us in every respect and yet never so different as to belong to another species. Just as some people make the error of grossly exaggerating racial and class distinctions, so it is possible for a certain kind of historian grossly to exaggerate the differences between generations, centuries and epochs. Thus, for example, we talk about medieval man, renaissance man and modern man, as

[1] Ecclesiastes 1. 9.

though these were almost different kinds of animal; and, of course, the differences are undeniably significant, but never quite so significant as the astonishing persistences and resemblances. Indeed, without these persistences and resemblances and the kind of intuitive understanding which they render possible, the distinctive characteristics of history A as a form of knowledge would hardly be possible.

But as well as constants of a physical, biological and psychological character the philosopher of history needs also to take into account the possibility, about which so many men, including both philosophers and historians, are firmly convinced, of a constant of a metaphysical, perhaps religious character without which there would not be any history at all, and certainly apart from which our history B would be a very different thing from what it is and has been. Of course this may be very variously conceived. A Marxist may define a dialectic of history which controls all historical events; a naturalistic atheist may talk about laws of history analogous to the supposed laws of nature; each in his own way elaborating some deterministic theme, some brooding element of fatality running through all things from whose control the course of events can never escape. Theists, on the other hand, will talk of the purpose and will of God, of a providence which creates and respects but nevertheless in its own subtle way governs our freedom, so that man in history is ultimately limited and overruled not by impersonal purposes deriving from the interior, impersonal forces beneath him, but by an absolute Personality located in the realm of reality above him.

This last approach raises a question especially important for theologians. Those who are most of all concerned with the divine reality will tell us that God is not in time, that his being is not a temporal being. God has no history and yet he is revealed in history, his purposes are worked out in history, and he is so related to the whole course of history that it can never be possible to deal with the course of history philosophically without taking the divine initiative most carefully into account. From this point of view the reality of God will be the supreme constant to which the many variables in history are always inescapably relative. Thus the philosophy of history cannot evade the great questions of the definition of eternity and of the relation of eternity to time. For it is this relation of the temporal to the will, the purpose, the knowledge and the love of the eternal which lends to the temporal its crucial and dramatic character. It is from this relationship to the eternal that the temporal derives its supreme significance. Indeed, for the theist it is because and only because of this relationship to the eternal that the temporal is. It pleased the eternal that the temporal should be. The implications of this statement tell us, if we are philosophical theologians, a great deal about the eternal, but perhaps, if we are historians or philosophers of history, they tell us even more about the temporal. Indeed, they tell us, and this is a strange paradox, that the *temporalia* eternally matter, that they pass but have an ultimate significance, that they perish one after the other but yet have an eternal destiny and purpose. For the moment, however, we must return to our concept of revelation.

In giving our brief outline of this modern concept of revelation, according to which God reveals himself in the coincidence of certain particular historical events with a prophetic interpretation of these events that perceives and declares their meaning, we see at once that this implies a philosophy of history according to which it is possible for events to have a meaning intrinsic to themselves. This notion that events can have, at least sometimes, an intrinsic objective meaning of their own, which men may perceive but cannot conceivably manufacture, must be carefully distinguished from two other doctrines which have also played some part in our intellectual history. Of course, it is true that any clear description of past events considered simply as a set of ascertainable facts will be a meaningful description. But the meaning of the event must be carefully distinguished from the meaningfulness of the description. There is no reason why a meaningless event should not nevertheless be meaningfully described. Just as it is possible for psychiatrists to give a rational account of irrational behaviour, so it would be possible for history A to give a meaningful description of a totally meaningless series of events. Many historians of a positivistic cast of mind would be quite content with this situation. Events, they would say, have no objective or intrinsic meaning of their own, or if they have, the historical methodology is quite incapable of grasping it; history must humbly confine itself to the lucid and meaningful description of ultimately meaningless facts. This is quite a clear point of view but it invokes a positivistic philosophy of history that would make our concept of revelation quite impossible. We may notice that it is quite compatible with the purely oracular doctrine of revelation found in so many forms of religion, but it is altogether contrary to any biblical concept of revelation.

Here we may note in passing that positivism does not, as so many people suppose, make religion and religious faith impossible. In fact, there are plenty of pious positivists. Positivism presents religion with a far more subtle danger than that. By casting doubt on the very possibility of rational theology and metaphysics it compels religion to be unintelligent, but not necessarily non-existent. From the point of view of positivism rational atheism is as absurd as rational theism, yet at the same time irrational theism is almost certainly more attractive to our instincts, more creative of historical vitality than irrational atheism. So long as positivism continues there will certainly be plenty of religious positivists, and from their own point of view quite rightly. The trouble about the religion of the positivist is that it is condemned to irrationality, for in such spheres as these, reason's writ, according to the positivist, does not run.

Now it is my conviction, and therefore the conviction which underlies this book, that the Christian tradition cannot tolerate the scandal of irrational, untheological religion. If this is so, an event like Christianity will have important philosophical presuppositions and implications, and one of these is precisely that events can have, and that some of them certainly do have, an intrinsic, objective, observable meaning of their own, so that Christianity places a pressure upon the philosophy of history to discover precisely how this can be the case. In other words, our doctrine of revelation implies a certain kind of philosophy of history, according to which some events at least, perhaps although not certainly all events, have an intrinsic, objective meaning of their own. Again, it would be generally agreed that it is always possible for men to give events a meaning which they need not intrinsically possess. The imaginative observer can read into events a symbolic import, sometimes it seems almost any symbolic import he pleases, so that historical events can be exhibited as the bearers of the meaning which he chooses to give to them.

In the history of biblical interpretation this is what we mean by allegory. Given sufficient ingenuity almost any story can be turned into an allegory made to mean what it does not intrinsically mean by the fanciful imagination of the narrator. It is undeniable that considered as a literary form this allegorization of events can often be a vehicle of great aesthetic and intellectual power. The allegorist may use his allegories to say very important and profoundly true things, but always it is he, the allegorist, who uses the events, who says these things. The events themselves, apart from the allegorist and his imaginative handling of them, say nothing at all. The great allegorists are interpreters of history and mythology, who make history and mythology a means of expressing their own philosophy, possibly a philosophy entirely alien to the mind of those who first gave us the histories and the myths. Thus Philo turns the events of the Old Testament into symbols of a more or less Hellenistic philosophy of life. The Genesis story has been used to symbolize many cosmologies, and in our own time Bultmann has used biblical events to symbolize the truth of what we may call a religious adaptation of Heidegger's existentialism, but there is an important distinction between observing the meaning intrinsic to an event and merely giving the event an extrinsic meaning which happens to appeal to us.

In Christian biblical interpretation we find side by side with allegory a quite distinct interpretative method which is often confused with it. Nowadays this is known as typology, and we may distinguish between the two by saying that whereas in allegory we give meanings to events, the aim of typology is that events should declare their meaning to us. In this book I shall be very much concerned to argue that biblical typology is a genuine historical method, particularly when carefully purged of all allegorical elements, and that in fact it is capable of being used much more widely than simply as a mode of biblical interpretation.

'History does not repeat itself.' This downright rejection of the familiar proverb is perhaps a truism rather than a truth. Every event is unique. Every event is this particular event, to be distinguished absolutely from any other. And yet we may observe, in the historical process, recurrent or analogous patterns in terms of which quite distinct groups of events can nevertheless be likened to each other and interpreted as illustrations of a single persistent historical theme. It is possible to select from world history distinct events all of which exemplify the same basic pattern, as a means of showing how persistently recurrent and how radically characteristic of the historical process this particular pattern is. The events, although taking place under quite different conditions and widely dispersed in space and time, nevertheless belong together as an intelligible group, and to interpret them as such does indeed enrich our understanding of history.

In the modern world Toynbee is perhaps the chief example of this particular method. Many historians, of course, simply attempt to grasp and delineate one unique event after another in the dimension of its singularity, on the assumption that no event casts any light whatever upon the character or meaning of any other event. We may call this positivist historiography, but there is also a typological historiography which takes the view that the correct ascertaining and interpretation of the great persistent historical themes is the supreme task and duty of the historian. If we now think particularly of Toynbee, whose work has been so violently criticized by the positivist historians, as the great champion of this type of historiography, in the ancient world this was the method particularly characteristic of biblical interpretation. Biblical events were arranged serially, each embodying an analogous pattern, and biblical interpretation was not so much the interpretation of this or that event in its singularity as an exposition of the cumulative meaning of the patterns, usually regarded as reaching some kind of culmination or fulfilment in Christ. The earlier events were held to foreshadow the final or eschatological event, the Christ, and this final eschatological event was regarded as fulfilling the expectations aroused by the earlier events. We shall attempt a fuller discussion of these and other distinct types of historiography in the next chapter. The only point I want to make at this stage is that Toynbee in the twentieth century, perhaps without knowing it, certainly without asserting or claiming it, has in fact revived and used in relation to all history a method of historical interpretation originally employed by the biblical theologians of the early Church.

In the modern world it has become almost a commonplace to say that the Bible is a set of historical documents or evidences which, of course, ought to be interpreted and critically handled in precisely the same way as any other set of historical documents or evidences. This statement is true yet nevertheless ambiguous. Normally it has been taken to mean that what I would call the positivistic method of study and interpretation should be as sovereign in the modern world in relation to biblical interpretation as it has been in all other kinds of modern historiography. It could, however, mean that the methods traditionally found appropriate in the case of classical biblical interpretation should be used in the interpretation of all history. In the first case we reduce the Bible to history; in the second case we elevate all history to the status of a kind of Bible. In fact, however, because of the triumph of the positivist spirit, in modern historiography no doubt in a somewhat subdued form, we have usually taken it for granted that the first meaning of the dictum is the appropriate one, that biblical documents must be studied in precisely the same way as all other historical documents. If anyone had even dreamed of interpreting it the other way round he might have preferred to say that all other historical events should be interpreted in precisely the same way as biblical events, which is, in effect, what Toynbee really does.

Yet, although distinct, these two methods of approach to history are not really so independent of each other as at first sight appears. It is possible to have positive history without any typological interpretation, but hardly possible to have typological history without a foundation of critical positive history. Thus Toynbee at least claims to begin where the positive historians leave off. In fact, of course, they never do leave off, and this is perhaps the chief cause of the many criticisms aimed against him. Still, we must have a positive critical account of events in their singularity in order to perceive that they really do embody and exemplify analogous historical patterns. Toynbee is usually criticized on the grounds that again and again his positive history is shaky, that the account he gives of events in order to show that they do indeed exemplify the patterns which he discovers in them, is often a misleading one. No doubt this is sometimes true, but Toynbee, or some ardent disciple of Toynbee's, is always entitled to reply that even though the method may here and there, or even everywhere, have been wrongly used, it is nevertheless the right method. After all, it was never pretended that this was an easy method, only that it was a necessary one.

In history, as in many of the natural sciences, we are constantly searching for methods capable of yielding accurate and valuable results which do not call for excessive amounts of individual talent or genius. Methodology, we may say, is modern man's substitute for genius. It may, of course, be doubted whether in the long run there is any substitute for genius, either in history, or in the natural sciences, or anywhere else. The subjective value is always implicit even in the most objective results. There are no methodologies which will enable mediocre men to produce the same results as great ones. Genius is not an infinite capacity for taking pains. If it were every painstaking mediocrity would look like a genius, which is very far from being the case. On the other hand, it must always be true that brilliant and insightful interpretation, whether of biblical events or of all historical events, must always rest upon a careful application of critical positive methods. It may go beyond them—indeed, it certainly will—but it can never altogether dispense with them.

24

In modern biblical controversies the great error has been that of those theologians who so often seem to suppose that they can get back to the basic biblical truth, not by going beyond modern critical studies of scripture, but rather by retreating from them and denying their utility altogether. The fundamentalists have tried to react against a real scandal, a method of interpreting a supremely great religious-historical document like the Bible out of which no word from God ever seems to come, a method which can give us more and more good positive history without in any way deepening our spiritual understanding. This is the inevitable result of plunging the biblical documents into the context of modern positive historical studies, without allowing the Bible itself to teach us anything at all about the historical methods by means of which it is interpreted. The product of such activity is a rather unsuccessful blend of a historical view of the Bible with a non- or at least sub-biblical view of history. I want to insist that the Bible has to be interpreted in the light of the Bible's own insights as to the nature of history and historical method, and that, indeed, all historical events must finally be interpreted in the same way. Instead of trying to be historical about the Bible—in the modern positivistic sense of the word historical—we must try to be biblical about history, and thus discover a new sense of the word historical or rather rediscover an old one. In the twentieth century Toynbee has come nearer to doing this than anyone else. I would not, of course, wish by any means to endorse everything that Toynbee has to say about history. It is his methodology rather than his conclusions which I am concerned to defend. I regard the contemporary fundamentalist protest against the comparative spiritual poverty and theological sterility of modern biblical scholarships as justified, but I think the protest is made in the wrong way and on the wrong grounds.

Perhaps we may conclude by noting that the concept of revelation embraced in this chapter entirely transforms the traditional controversy about the relation of reason to revelation. What I have called the oracular doctrine of revelation inevitably led to a head-on collision between theologians on the one hand and rationalist philosophers and metaphysicians on the other. The oracular doctrine of revelation is inevitably a scandal and a stumbling block to the rationalist metaphysician. We may imagine a picket line of philosophers parading up and down outside the cathedral with banners reading: 'Unfair to professional philosophers! Undemonstrated metaphysical propositions being uttered here!' For, after all, the alleged biblical oracles were given something of the character of metaphysical propositions, and it was certainly supposed by many theologians either that they could not rationally be demonstrated, or that even if they could they were never to be accepted by the faithful on precisely those grounds. Once we have grasped, however, that the proper task of reason is the interpretation of experience, and that revelation is itself a form of experience given to us in history, then it becomes plain that revelation is something to be reasoned about just as much as any other form of experience, and the old controversy becomes meaningless and dead. Indeed, the battle between revelation and reason becomes simply an aspect of the old struggle between rationalism and empiricism in philosophy.

Revelationism in religion, we may say, is the theological counterpart of empiricism in philosophy. Revelation is no more a substitute for reason in theology than plants and flowers are a substitute for reason in botany. Revelation is the datum which religious or theological reasoning is constrained to interpret, just as the life and behaviour of plants and flowers is interpreted by botany. Religion like metaphysics can never be the product of mere rational speculation. In both theology and metaphysics the meaning of the term to be used must be grounded in genuine experience. Religious knowledge like all other forms of knowledge, is rooted in our rational intercourse with events, an intercourse which first sees events as they are and then analytically shows what they imply and what they presuppose. In the same way religion itself is grounded upon events, is indeed an interpretation of events, of certain particular events, regarded as peculiarly crucial for the solution of the problems which are being considered, and then of all other events in the light of these interpretations. It is the interpretation of the crucial events which provides us with our basic theological ideas. It is the interpretation of all other events in the light of these basic theological ideas which verifies their adequacy and power.

It will be noticed that no particular empirical inquiry ever investigates all experience taken as a whole. Each particular inquiry begins by observing that some particular stream in or strand of experience is crucial in relation to the main problem. Problems in physics cannot be solved by a course of psychological or historical research, nor are all physical events by any means equally relevant to any one physical problem. This after all is just as well. If we had to examine the whole of experience before venturing upon any particular empirical conclusion, our empiricism would never get off the ground. Similarly historical events are not all equally relevant to any particular historical question. In that branch of history which we call Christian theology—for despite all that affiliates it to metaphysics it is, nevertheless, in its own peculiar way a branch of history—certain events, those to which the Bible testifies, are taken to be crucial. It is from the interpretation of the scriptures that we derive the key theological ideas. But, of course, once we have derived them we can only verify them by using them as the clues

27

to the interpretation of all history, indeed, our whole experience of human existence.

Revelation in religion is thus the theological counterpart of empiricism in philosophy, for revelation after all is no more than an abstract noun which both connotes and denotes the whole class of revelatory events. It is with the interpretation of this class of concrete events that the theologian is entrusted.

We must beware, however, of making the category of revelation so peculiarly religious and theological that it has no *locus standi* in any other discipline. The fact is that all experience is in some degree revelational, in so far as every experience is revelatory of itself. The extent to which some experiences at least are revelatory not only of themselves but also of that ultimate reality which religion is concerned to love and theology to understand is one to which we must pay more careful attention in the following chapters.

APPENDIX TO CHAPTER 1

A NOTE ON PROCESS PHILOSOPHY AND NEO-ORTHODOX THEOLOGY

THE reference in chapter 1 to process philosophy and neo-orthodox theology is perhaps the kind of thing that is all very well in a lecture but scarcely permissible in a printed book. However, it hardly seemed practical to introduce a lengthy digression on these subjects into the text itself, and so it is that I venture to provide a short summary of my rather critical and negative reactions to these species of doctrine in a rather more lengthy appended note.

1. *The so-called* 'Process' *Philosophy:* This type of philosophy, which except here and there in America is now somewhat *passé*, is derived from the justly celebrated work of the late Professor Whitehead, although he was hardly a process philosopher in the sense in which many of his disciples used that term. With the possible exception of Bergson, he is the most celebrated example of a tendency in some post-Darwinian thinkers to be more influenced by biology than by physics. The extent to which the purely biological hypothesis of evolution was transformed into a philosophical doctrine in post-Darwinian thought has not perhaps been noticed or discussed quite so much as it deserves. For example, the term evolution in Bergson means something quite different from anything that it meant in Darwin or means in the work of contemporary biologists. In fact, it came to mean something remarkably akin to divine immanence, a kind of restless spirit making for novelty and change deep down in the heart of all things. This was not altogether unlike the picture of God in Christian theology. We might say that it did justice to half the Christian picture, for God in Christian doctrine certainly is immanent. But to the transcendent aspect of the picture it did, of course, no justice at all. It was very close, however, to some kinds of mysticism, and easily assimilated by those Christian writers

earlier in this century who laid especial stress on what they called 'religious experience.'

The resulting doctrine of the universe, however, had more in common with the speculations of the pre-Socratic Greek philosopher, Heraclitus. The universe, according to this doctrine, is really a process of all comprehending change. Everything in it is striving and straining towards change, and sooner or later it is successful in its seeking. Thus process rather than being is the primary characteristic of the universe. The word *God* no longer means the being of God, but rather the process of creating the world. Similarly the word *man* no longer refers to the being of man, but rather to the process of being human, which is really the process of gradually becoming something else. The very idea of being was decried as 'static' and there was tremendous enthusiasm for more dynamic concepts, which were sometimes supposed to be closer to the spirit of the Bible and to the Hebrew idea of the living God. This was seized upon with particular enthusiasm by theologians who were anxious to proclaim their loyalty to the spirit of the Bible as reconstructed by modern scholars, and at the same time to find in, or read into, the Bible reasons for departing entirely from the doctrines and dogmas found in classical Christian theology, both patristic and medieval. In this way they could seem far more radically protestant and anti-catholic than even the great protestant reformers themselves.

Of course, we post-Darwinians can hardly escape being influenced by the concept of evolution, nor have we any reason for even wishing to do so. We now know that creation is by evolution, and that is to us the inscrutable way in which God has chosen to operate. There may still to us be profound difficulties about evolution but, in the celebrated words of Cardinal Newman, 'Ten thousand difficulties don't make one doubt.' Nevertheless, there is no reason why we should be more influenced in philosophy by the doctrine of evolution than by other great scientific hypotheses. For example, the principle of inertia, or resistance to change, would appear to be just as characteristic of the creation as the principle of evolution. It would appear that many things in the universe do not evolve, and even if they did once emerge in the evolutionary way they seem to have settled down in their place and remained where they are ever since. Thus, even if we suppose that, primitively, organisms emerged out of a purely inorganic world, it is still plainly the case that most inorganic realities have remained inorganic. Indeed, it is only because the inorganic has remained inorganic that it has been possible for organisms to flourish and survive. By and large, we must say that things do not display this reckless appetite for change which has been attributed to them. On the contrary, things are pressured to change reluctantly by the force of exceptional circumstances. Even then most of them do not change but apparently prefer to die. Resistance to change and unreadiness to change is apparently as characteristic of reality as the capacity to evolve. Even to-day this is true of human life and of personal and social development, as we know them in politics, in social history and in individual personality. It is a misreading of reality to suppose that it is merely or only a story of evolution.

Whitehead himself was more influenced by the idea of organism than by the idea of evolution. He was thinking in a world in which a more or less mechanistic type of science had attempted to reduce organic processes simply to a rather complicated kind of inorganic process. The characteristic eighteenth-century analogy likened the Newtonian universe to a very complicated machine, and then, since it is always the way of naïve and unphilosophical minds to literalize images and analogies—as we see, for example, in fundamentalism—it proceeded to think of the universe as though it really were a machine. We may say that the mechanisitc interpreters of science were really scientific fundamentalists, crassly mistaking an analogy for a fact. The result was a mechanistic biology that Whitehead felt really would not do. He proposed that we should reverse the formula. Instead of interpreting organic processes as very complicated examples of inorganic process, we should rather treat the inorganic as a primitive and simple instance of the organic. Thus he conceived the whole universe as in some sense alive.

We may say that this is another example of what we may call a 'one-stuff' philosophy. It is characteristically Greek, indeed, pre-Socratic. But we find in the modern world examples of it in idealism and materialism and in the 'neutral stuff' theory of Bertrand Russell. The ancient Greek thinkers were very anxious to show that, despite the plurality of gods and goddesses in Greek mythology, the cosmos was, nevertheless, one universe because it was all made out of the same basic stuff. Actually the pagan mythologies provided the germ of this idea in their notion that the universe was originally created out of chaos. Although the many things in the universe differ from each other so sharply, really they are all created out of the same elementary material. The universe is thus one universe.

Christian monotheism, however, had an entirely different solution for this basic problem. The universe is one universe because it is all created by one God, and therefore not created out of any basic stuff at all. Thus Christian thought could take the obvious differences between things far more seriously than Greek thought was able to do, because it no longer supposed that the unity of the universe depended upon any doctrine of an elementary basic stuff. This is perhaps the most important departure of Christian thought from Greek thought, and it is quite remarkable how little has been made of it in the conventional histories of western intellectual development.

The Renaissance and post-Renaissance reaction against Christian thought has again and again reverted to some form or other of this characteristically Greek idea of some one elementary basic stuff. Thus, according to the idealist, all is mind and what we usually look upon as matter or material process is really mental process in a very simple and uncomplicated form. According to the materialists all is matter, and what we usually look upon as mind is simply material process in a very complicated form. Bertrand Russell offered us the doctrine of a 'neutral stuff' which is neither matter nor mind, but which can be interpreted as either according to our subjective point of view or purpose. According to the mechanists all processes are basically inorganic, and organic process is simply inorganic process in a highly complicated form. According to Whitehead all is organic, and inorganic process is merely organic process in a very simple form. For myself I feel the same objection to all 'one-stuff' theories, and, as a theist, I feel able to say to each in turn, 'I have no need of that hypothesis.' For me the unity of the creation is based upon the common relationship which all creatures have to their creator and not upon an idea of an elementary basic stuff. Of course, from the point of view of biblical and Christian theism, there was no basic elementary stuff, just as, for that matter, there was no plurality of elementary basic stuffs. The creation was not created out of anything that preceded the creation. From this point of view all 'one-stuff' theories are false and misleading, and all propositions of the form, 'In the last analysis everything is X,' must therefore be denied. This doctrine has at least the advantage of setting us free to recognize and enjoy the extraordinary variety of the things that confront us in actual experience. Hence I would reject the Whiteheadian doctrine, not so much because of anything peculiar to itself, but because of a point of view which it shares with many other doctrines, all of which it seems to me necessary to reject in the same way.

But to the process philosophy itself I would add an ethical objection to which I would attach even greater importance. The tendency to substitute the idea of process for the idea of beings and things appears to me to be fatal to our civilized ethical traditions. In Christian thought the tendency has always been to move from function to status. Thus Jesus Christ did not merely perform messianic functions, he was the Messiah. We do not say that he was the Messiah because he performed messianic functions, but rather that he performed messianic functions because he was the Messiah. Again, the ordained minister of the church is not merely a man who performs ministerial functions, he is a priest. We do not say that he is a priest because he performs priestly functions, but, on the contrary, that he performs priestly functions because he is a priest. Beings have a dignity of their own. They can be honoured, loved and served. But functions can only be used, perhaps exploited. So long as we think of a man as a process or a function, we shall never really think of him as a man. Being has a dignity, a meaning, and value intrinsic to itself, which mere process can never attain. Woe betide man and civilization if ever we get into the habit of thinking of men as mere processes and functions. And what is to become of worship and prayer if we get into the habit of thinking of God in this crass, impersonal way.

In another, more existentialist, sense, of course, being itself is the supreme process, the highest activity of all. To be, as we see it in the being of God, to transcend utterly all time and change, to affirm the fullness of oneself immutably—so that we can say to God, in the words of the Bible, 'Thou art the same, and thy years shall not fail'—this is activity indeed. We are too much accustomed to that helpless and supine acquiescence in mere change which we may call changing and interpret in terms of restless activity, but which is in fact far more like being changed than changing. The immense and immutable self-affirmation which we find in the being of God, this, after all, is what the extentialists long for as they philosophize neurotically in the jaws of death, and it is this kind of existence that the Christian gospel promises and proclaims.

2. *Neo-Orthodox Theology:* The alleged orthodoxy of the so-called neo-orthodox is not orthodoxy in the normal or catholic sense of the word. In this classical, normative sense the term orthodoxy refers primarily to the great decisions about Christ, the Holy Spirit, and the Trinity, which emerged out of the searching theological debates and inquiries that took place in the church in the first five centuries of its existence. In this classical, normative sense the great reformers and the early protestants were entirely orthodox. The so-called neo-orthodoxy, however, is not necessarily a return to classical Christology and the doctrine of the Trinity. It is really a reaction against nineteenth-century forms of liberal protestantism which denied the doctrines of the fall and original sin. What it reacted towards was the somewhat extreme version of those doctrines which we find in the writings of St. Augustine and above all in Calvin. In many areas of thought Christian orthodoxy does not indicate any one doctrine, but rather what may be described as a spectrum of belief, so that anything that falls within the spectrum can be regarded as orthodox. There is in Christian history no official dogma of the fall and original

sin, but a number of distinct doctrines all of which affirm them and attempt to interpret them. Thus there is much in the catholic tradition which many protestants, including the neo-orthodox, would describe, somewhat unfairly, as semi-Pelagian. Man cannot get along without God, and God, the creator of man and the dignity of his freedom, will not get along without man. The neo-orthodox take this to mean that the germ of the fallacies of optimistic liberalism about man is to be found even in the catholic tradition itself.

Thus the 'orthodoxy' of the neo-orthodox is really an extreme Calvinistic interpretation of the fall and original sin which, although orthodox in the sense of being within the permitted spectrum of belief—although right at one end of it—ought nevertheless not to be regarded as in any sense uniquely definitive of orthodoxy. For example, this extreme doctrine is practically unknown in eastern Orthodoxy. To all catholic Christians, therefore, protestant neo-orthodoxy is unacceptable because the content of its alleged orthodoxy is not theological and Christological, but anthropological, and this, as it seems to them, is to put the cart before the horse. On the other hand, to many protestants of more or less fundamentalist persuasion, the characteristic conviction of protestant orthodoxy is the doctrine of the verbal inspiration of the scriptures, so that to them also neo-orthodoxy is not really orthodox.

From the standpoint of contemporary apologetics we may add this: Distrust of man and humanism, and despair of all human prospects, is not really a reason for believing and trusting in God. After all, many contemporary existentialists share the despair of the neo-orthodox about man's desperate plight, but they do not for that reason turn to God. Many of them think it more courageous to persevere in eloquent despair, with, as they pride themselves, greater integrity and more magnificent fortitude. Certainly the condition of man without God is a desperate one, but, under the fall, even the condition of man with God, man armed with his faltering and spasmodic faith, is, to say the least, extremely precarious. God has made himself known in his Word, and in the Church has created for us a context of existence and a form of experience in and through which we can receive his Word and glory in it. But even man under the Word, man in the Church, is still fallen man with all the dangers and calamities that that implies. God is not a desperate last resort, nor the Church a funk-hole. On the contrary, God must always be our first resort and the Church the temple of our glory. The great neo-orthodox theologians have many extraordinary gifts, and their writings abound with profound insights, but the term neo-orthodoxy itself is a very misleading one, certainly from the standpoint of anything that can properly be called orthodoxy. We cannot say that the heart of the gospel is the doctrine of man, or a speculative interpretation of the mode and manner of human salvation.

Chapter 2

TYPES OF HISTORIOGRAPHY

WE have already in our last chapter made several references to what I have called positivist historiography. I think it should be admitted that in its extreme, rigorously logical form a purely positivist historiography is very rare. There are many approaches to it, but it remains a kind of ideal type to which very few writers entirely conform. A purely positivist historiography would take the view that every historical episode is an entirely singular event, that no historical episode logically implies any other, so that, however completely we apprehend it, it provides us with no information whatever about any other episode, and that neither in itself nor in conjunction with our knowledge of other episodes can it serve as the basis for any general conclusions about the historical process as a whole. Thus historical knowledge about a particular event A is simply knowledge of event A, nothing less, nothing more. This knowledge is made possible by such evidences of events in past time as still survive and are available in present time. The most important of these consist of written documents, inscriptions, etc., but there may also be other forms of evidence, particularly those made available by archaeological research. Historical knowledge is simply knowledge of particular facts and no transition is possible to any more general understanding of the peculiar type of process in the context of which such facts occur.

This type of historiography is in violent conflict with anything which might properly be called philosophy of history. Yet it is itself a kind of philosophy, although I think a bad one. It often professes to regard itself as peculiarly scientific, no doubt because of its purely empirical way of handling evidences, but we may question whether it really deserves so exalted an adjective. Except in the very early stage, in which it is busy collecting facts and recognizing its data, science is not primarily a knowledge of facts, but primarily an understanding of processes and a devising of theories. Our purely positivist history makes a virtue of not even trying to understand processes and never venturing upon anything which could be called a theory. From this point of view we can describe a purely positivistic concept of historiography and historical method as a radically unscientific one whose basic dogma is that no science of history is possible.

Yet although in this sense positivistic history makes any science or philosophy impossible, that does not mean that it has no philosophical affiliations, presuppositions or implications. On the contrary, positivist history is one aspect of a very important philosophical movement. We may say that its affiliations are with late mediaeval nominalism and eighteenth-century British empiricism, which are two closely related and very similar philosophical movements. One way of discovering the similarity is to compare William of Occam and his followers with David Hume. It is impossible not to be struck by the way in which all the basic nominalist ideas—I almost said errors—recur in the Humian philosophy. Everything is simply what it is and nothing implies anything about anything else. This is why both philosophies have so much difficulty with any concept of causality. If there is any reality at all corresponding to our notion of causality, then it must surely be the case that some things at least do imply conclusions about the state of other things.

Causality, which in the nineteenth century seemed to be the key scientific concept, has rather fallen by the wayside in the twentieth century, and it now appears that there is much to be said for a formulation of physical

38

theory that at least avoids using the concept of causality. After all, we derive our vivid concept of causality from our own experience of acting causally, our experience of ourselves as causal agents. There is thus much to be said for the view that to read this notion of causality into physical science is a crude anthropomorphism which the progress of mathematical physics may very well eliminate. If I say that one physical state of affairs is the cause of another physical state of affairs I am really implying that it exerts a power or influence over it analogous to the power or influence a man may exercise over the pen which he causes to inscribe certain particular sentences on a piece of paper. In other words, to talk about causality in physics is a kind of last relic of Greek polytheism, which peoples the cosmos with occult spiritual forces or gods. There is thus much to be said for the view that physics not only should but must get rid of the concept of causality.

But when we are dealing with history, with the careers of beings like ourselves, who are aware and often vividly aware of exercising causal influence not only on themselves and each other but also upon things, we may very well question whether it can ever be feasible to abandon the concept of causality. History, after all, is the story of the acts and careers of the only beings in the cosmos of whom we can say that we know for certain that they do indeed act causally. Surely in the case of history the causal category is a manifest necessity. A theory of history which isolates one event from another finds itself paralysed before it begins. But this leads us to doubt whether, at least in the special case of history, it can really be true that the knowledge of one event tells us nothing whatever about any other event. History really is, we might say, what we used wrongly to think natural science is, purely empirical and radically causal. Science, on the other hand, is mathematical and functional rather than causal, and only empirical in its techniques of verification.

Of course, part of the trouble here is the ambiguity of the term *empiricism*. Empiricism may mean, as perhaps it did to Newton, that our hypotheses are implied by the phenomena they are designed to interpret. From this point of view science is supposed to study and analyse the facts with which it is confronted until the facts themselves seem to suggest and imply the more general notions in terms of which they can be rationally comprehended and understood. The scientist concentrates his unwearying gaze upon the facts with which he is concerned until at last he perceives what they imply. This is perhaps what Newton meant when he said *Hypotheses non fingo*. From our point of view this claim would seem flagrantly untrue, and we rightly talk about the Newtonian hypothesis, although Newton perhaps genuinely believed that his hypothesis really was implied by the facts it was supposed to interpret. But we now know for certain, indeed, it is almost a commonplace, that this interpretation is incorrect, that such an account of the role of the mind in scientific advances is altogether inadequate and misleading. Science is a work of the imagination, of bold speculative leaps analogous to those which we find in the great metaphysicians.

Yet we should rightly say that science is never purely speculative, and this is because it has built up techniques of empirical and experimental verification that enable us to distinguish between bold speculative leaps which are valuable and others which are worthless. It is precisely because the facts do not imply the hypotheses which interpret them that we have had to build up these techniques of verification. If it could be shown that scientific hypotheses are implied by the facts they interpret, then verification would be unnecessary.

This brings us to the second possible meaning of the term *empirical*. Science is empirical because it employs empirical methods of verification. 'If my hypothesis H is correct,' says the experimental scientist, 'then under conditions X I should observe phenomenon Y.' Such a calculation enables the investigator to formulate his crucial experiment, in which he carefully sets up conditions X in order to ascertain whether or not Y is observable. If Y is not observable he rightly concludes that hypothesis H is either incorrect or at least incorrectly formulated. If Y is observable this certainly does not prove that H is correct, indeed, in the proper logical and mathematical sense of the word *proof*, there is no such thing as a scientific proof. If Y is observed as calculated, then the probability that H is correct is certainly increased, and H may become part of what we may call accepted scientific orthodoxy, at least until an even better hypothesis is formulated to take its place. From this point of view the experimental method is the true essence of empiricism.

A third possible sense of the term *empirical* revolves round the difference between pure concepts and what might be termed conceptualized percepts. Universal or general terms like *white* or *horse* represent a mere conceptualization arrived at by a process of abstraction from items given to us in immediate experience. On the other hand, we are aware of and use certain other concepts, like causality or the square root of minus two, which are never concretely embodied in experience. In some cases, causality for example, we may say that we do enjoy experiences in terms of which we can give meaning to these concepts, not by abstraction but rather by analogy. For example, although we have no percept corresponding to and conceptualized by our idea of causality, we are aware that we ourselves again and again in life act causally, and by analogy we may be able to locate some similar causal power elsewhere in the universe, either in things or in God or in both. When I speak of analogy I do not mean the so-called 'argument from analogy' to which a chapter, usually a somewhat critical one, is devoted in many textbooks of logic. Analogy is not an argument, but a way of giving meaning to pure concepts which do not conceptualize any percept vouchsafed to us in immediate experience, but which, on the other hand, can nevertheless be shown to be not altogether foreign to our experience. I would say that analogy is a technique by means of which we impart a certain 'empirical resonance' to a pure concept. Analogy is particularly at home in the realms of theology and metaphysics, where we constantly have to employ concepts which at first sight would appear to possess no empirical resonance at all, so that many critics of theology and metaphysics can plausibly argue that the characteristic concepts of these disciplines are mere meaningless words.

Empiricism in this third sense may be an insistence that the only concepts permissible in science and philosophy are conceptualized percepts, so that pure concepts would be banned altogether. No doubt this is very close to what is sometimes called phenomenalism, and to most varieties of modern positivism. It is, however, very distant from modern science, which in its highly mathematical phases finds itself constantly driven to the employment of pure concepts.

Relativity, for example, is pure concept of this kind. Of course, we know that the basic idea of relativity is given to us by a common, indeed everyday, experience. Every observation and impression is modified by the point of view of the observer, particularly by his ethical and social prejudices. But relativity is no mere conceptualization of this experience; relativity in physics has nothing to do with what is called relativism in ethics. Relativism merely accepts the brute fact of the dependence of the observation on the point of view of the observer, jumps to the conclusion that there must consequently be a subjective element in every judgement, and from this derives the further conclusion that pure objectivity is impossible, with somewhat disastrous consequences for ethics. *Relativity*, on the other hand, reaches a pure concept by the process of analogy and uses the very fact that *relative* judgements occur as an objective insight into the nature of the field in which such judgements occur, so that in the end our recognition of the fact of *relativity* conducts us further towards an objective knowledge of our situation. The difference between *relativity* in physics and *relativism* in ethics is thus very considerable. It is, indeed, the difference between arriving at a pure concept by analogy and merely conceptualizing a percept by a process of abstraction.

Behind this possible meaning of empiricism, this insistence that only conceptualized percepts can be admitted into a theoretical structure, there lies the implication that the system of percepts is a closed and self-explanatory system, and this implication is open to the gravest doubt. No satisfactory account of the world of experience can possibly be given simply in terms of itself, or, to use our present terminology, the interpretation of percepts in terms of conceptualized percepts cannot amount to a rational interpretation of experience. If the percepts themselves are not self-explanatory, the mere conceptualization of the percepts will not suffice to make them so. This is one way of insisting on the necessity of metaphysics, and at least the possibility of theology.

Now in the second of our three possible senses of the term empirical history is not and never can be empirical, for history is not experimental, but it is possible for the historian to be empirical, or at least to try to be empirical in the first and third senses. He may insist on entertaining no notions of a general character except those which are directly and inescapably implied by the data, or he may at least insist on purging his system of all pure concepts and employing no concepts except such as can plausibly be shown to be conceptualized percepts, as, for example, in descriptive and practical economics. If, however, he decides to be empirical in this sense, it is doubtful whether he can succeed in being purely positivistic, for he will constantly find himself confronted with historical evidences, memoirs, autobiographies, cabinet decisions, letters concerning matters of high policy, etc., in which historical characters clearly assert their intention to perform certain actions or to embark on certain policies in order that certain foreseen, calculated and predicted consequences may result. Bismarck composes a certain telegram in order to force France to declare war on Germany, a result which tragically comes to pass. Thus we cannot say, in extreme positivistic fashion, that the episode of Bismarck's telegram has nothing to do with and casts no light upon the French declaration of war. We can hardly avoid using the term causality in this case, although we hasten to notice that when the term causality is properly employed any suggestion of a kind of deterministic fatefulness has to be rejected. After all, the telegram did not compel the French to declare war on Germany; it influenced them to do so in some more subtle and less violent fashion. But at least the hypothesis that France declared war on Germany in 1870 because Bismarck wrote his telegram is one suggested if not altogether implied by the known facts. (I am not, of course, for one moment suggesting that this is an entirely adequate account of the event in question. If a historical event is caused it must at least be granted that it may have a plurality of causes. No one event is caused by any one other event, but by a large number of distinct events, all converging to exercise their causal influence at a particular moment and place.)

We conclude from this discussion that positivistic history can hardly be called scientific history. It may have its measure of empiricism, but its empiricism is hardly the refined empiricism of modern science. Rather it is the crude empiricism of modern science in its earlier phases.

Again, positivistic history is related not only to nominalism and to eighteenth-century empiricism but also to a peculiar kind of phenomenalism. According to this view nothing is real or need be taken into either historical or scientific account except observable phenomena. Any possible distinction between *real* and *actual* is ignored. Of course, from this point of view, not all phenomena are in fact observed, but they are all in principle observable. The only reality is phenomenal reality. More subtle, flexible accounts of reality, according to which it includes not only phenomenal and historical actuality but also other modes of being real like potentiality, not only the stark fact of existence but also subsistence, are rejected by this crude and brutal kind of philosophizing. Reality is reduced to actuality, and nothing else is taken into account at all. Again, naïve philosophies of this kind once drew their strength from the widespread supposition that, however crude and blindly unmetaphysical they might be, they at least fitted in with the tone and temper of modern science, but in the twentieth century we can see clearly enough that this is not in fact the case. For much in modern physics what does not happen under certain circumstances may be quite as significant as what does happen. The ancient notion of potentiality, as Professor Heisenberg has pointed out, has been to a considerable extent reinstated in quantum physics by his own famous principle of indeterminacy. Similarly, the tendency to account for the movements of particles and the structure of events in terms of the laws of the field or context in which they take place is very like the old philosophical notion of subsistence. Historical phenomenalism takes the form of the doctrine that a man simply is what he does, or conversely what happens to him. According to this view a man is simply the class of his own acts. We can

45

find ideas of this kind widespread in modern philosophy, in the activism of John Dewey, for example, and in existentialist notions about a man creating himself by a series of decisions and actions in time. Man, we are told, 'is what he makes himself.' It may, of course, be true that man becomes what he makes of himself, but this is not quite the same thing. In fact, if reality is merely actuality it is not a self-sufficient system. There is more to reality than mere actuality, and hence more to history than a mere behaviouristic description of what men do. Man is not only what he does; he is also what he does not do. In fact, he is not the mere doing of this or the mere non-doing of that; he is always the being who does this and does not do that. In the long run the problem of history is not merely the problem of what man does or has done, it is the problem of what man *is*, and this is hardly the kind of problem with which a purely positivistic method can even begin to deal.

The appeal of this positivist historiography, as we have already noticed, is the widespread idea that a hard-boiled, purely factual approach to history will give it something of the character and prestige of the natural sciences. This, as we have seen, is due to a mistake about the nature of scientific thought, which is much more imaginative and speculative than is usually supposed. If the factual, positivist approach in history affiliates it with the natural sciences at all, it is only to the sciences as they appear to be at their earliest and crudest stage, not to the later and more impressive developments of scientific thought. Perhaps the prevalence of the popular errors about the nature of scientific thought is due to the persistent use of the verb *discover* in the popular chronicling of scientific achievements. Thus I have even seen Einstein described as the discoverer of relativity, whereas, in fact, of course, Einstein did not discover relativity; rather he invented and devised the theory of relativity—a very different thing. There are, of course, genuine scientific discoveries, like, for example, the observation of the planet Uranus, although even in that case the existence of the planet had been calculated before it was actually observed. The observation merely verified the calculation. Similarly there are genuine discoveries in history, such as, for example, the famous Dead Sea Scrolls; but the genius of science in its most developed form shows itself not in dramatic discoveries of this kind but in the capacity to build up theories and hypotheses which will enable us to calculate possibilities which can subsequently be observed as actualities.

In fact, however, the purely positivist, factual, almost behaviourist theory of historical research and of writing history has very rarely been carried out in actual practice. What we find in most cases is a recording of facts plus a considerable number of somewhat questionable psychological interpretations. History is just as much the history of human thoughts as the history of human actions, and almost all historians attempt to record not only human deeds but also the motives and purposes which at least in part determine them. 'Historical facts,' Mark Bloch tells us, 'are in essence psychological facts.'[1] However, he goes on to warn us that psychology cannot confine itself to pure consciousness, and adds, 'In view of the actual state of investigation into the life of the mind and its obscure depths, this is a further proof of the everlasting difficulty which the sciences experience in trying to remain contemporaneous with each other.'[2] The naïve psychology which accompanied nominalist philosophy reduced mind to consciousness, and we are now almost certain that mind cannot be reduced to consciousness. Bloch illustrates from a German history of the French Revolution: 'The Herbertists, one German historian writes, were at first in perfect accord with Robespierre because he yielded to all

[1] *The Historian's Craft*. Manchester University Press, 1954, p. 194.
[2] Ibid., p. 194.

47

their desires; then they broke with him because they considered him too powerful. This . . . is to imply the two following propositions: a favour provokes gratitude; people do not like to be dominated. Now, these two propositions are not necessarily false, to be sure. But neither are they necessarily true.'[1] Some people, in fact, like to be dominated, and St. Vincent de Paul once exhorted a disciple, 'always to love the poor; because only if we truly love the poor will they forgive us for having given them bread.' It is perhaps not surprising that so much positivistic history indulges in so much naïve psychology. The affiliation with philosophical phenomenalism accounts for the coincidence. Reality according to this doctrine is identical with actuality; mind is simply another name for consciousness. All that exists is either there in the clear light of day or at least capable of being brought into it. There are no mysteries: the mysterious is simply a misinterpretation of the unknown.

Nowadays, however, there is some attempt by historians to adopt a more Freudian method: to combine a more or less positivistic approach to historical facts with a less naïve psychology. There is, however, a snag about this also. The obvious difficulty is the impossibility of successfully psycho-analysing dead or even absent people. It is, after all, difficult enough to psycho-analyse successfully even living and present ones, and it is well known that different schools of psycho-analysis will interpret precisely the same data in diverse ways.

In any case, too great a concern with the images and fantasies which throng the unconscious and haunt the conscious can provide us with only a one-sided picture of human beings in actual operation. Of course, we all experience these images and fantasies. In some cases we are actually bemused and misled by them, but more often

[1] Ibid., p. 195.

48

men know that their fantasies are fantasies, and learn to treat them as such.

The distinction between the rational and the irrational man is not the distinction between the man who has fantasies and the man who has nothing of the kind, but rather the distinction between the man who is imposed upon by his fantasies and the man who recognizes his fantasies for what they are. It is a mistake to suppose that the development of analytic psychology has completely overthrown the old ideal of rational man. It has complicated it somewhat, but it is still true that human existence is a kind of tension between the rational and the irrational. The human being is neither wholly rational nor wholly irrational. The essence of rationality is not to be free from irrationality, but rather always to recognize one's irrationality for what it is and to evaluate it at its true worth. Thus, for example, we hear a good deal nowadays about the exploitation of psychological motifs in advertising and salesmanship. We are told that a large and imposing motor-car brings with it a suggestion of achievement and power, inflates the ego and symbolizes prosperity. The small sports car is suggestive of a dashing, devil-may-care personality. We are even told that the convertible suggests the mistress and has overtones of sexual gratification. Presumably the station wagon suggests the family and the fulfilled masculinity of the *pater familias*. But a man may be influenced by all these images and yet for sound economic reasons still prefer a small and compact car simply because the taxes are lower, and the mileage per gallon so much higher. We can have fantasies, in other words, even indulge them to some extent, and yet reject them because we know that we must make a rational decision.

Of course, all human existence is a psychological phenomenon, but we must not suppose that human existence takes place in a kind of psychological vacuum,

49

except perhaps in the case of some of the graver and more tragic psychotic states, which are perhaps the only purely psychological phenomena. Psychological events always take place in inescapable relation to non-psychological events. What man does is psychological, but what he does it in relation to and in response to is very often non-psychological. A man's emotion of fear when he finds himself trapped in a burning house is a psychological phenomenon, but the burning house itself is a non-psychological phenomenon. If the man is haunted by the fear of being trapped in a burning house when, in fact, there is nothing burning, that is not merely a psychological phenomenon, but also a pathological one. Oddly enough, the more purely psychological our states of mind are, the more pathological they are. Conversely, the less pathological states of mind are always a mixture of non-psychological stimulus and psychological response. Thus historical explanation can never be merely a matter of psychology, although at the same time it can never leave psychology out.

This is an important consideration when we are examining urgent contemporary problems, like juvenile delinquency. Of course, this is a problem which has important psychological aspects, but it is not the kind of problem which can safely and properly be handed over to the psychologist for solution. Juvenile delinquency is a response to conditions prevalent at a particular stage of social development. We have to ask ourselves what are the prevalent social conditions conducive to our present high juvenile delinquency rates. It is useless to talk in terms of psychological concepts like the *oedipus complex*, for these things presumably we have with us always, even when juvenile delinquency rates are low. The problem of juvenile delinquency is not merely the problem of the psychological condition of the delinquent, it is also the problem of a diseased social structure. This is because the problem of juvenile delinquency is not merely a matter of bringing psychological aid and counsel to the juvenile delinquents we have at present, but rather the problem of how so to reorder and reconstruct our social system that we shall have fewer delinquents in the future. The main concern is not with our present unruly teenagers but with infants, and indeed the unborn, who probably will be unruly teenagers very shortly unless we look to the shape and structure of the society in which they are to grow up. My point here is that if a purely psychological approach to the interpretation and understanding of the present events is manifestly inadequate, it must be equally inadequate to our interpretation of past events. Or, to put it in terms of a language which we adopted in our last chapter, while there are many psychological constants in the historical process, there are even more non-psychological constants, and both must be taken into account if we are to interpret history in any balanced fashion.

We have thus isolated and distinguished from each other three kindred types of historiography: (a) a purely positivist, behaviouristic historiography, which is very rare; (b) the same type of historiography plus a certain amount of naïve psychological interpretation—naïve because in effect it equates mind with consciousness; (c) a similar combination with a psychology of a more profound type which admits the notion of obscure, unconscious psychological factors operating in the unrecognized depths of the mind. Of these three the second has been by far the most commonly encountered, but the third, despite its difficulties and uncertainties, is rapidly advancing towards the first place. Our objection to the more profound type of psychological interpretation has been basically the same as our objection to the more naïve variety of the mode. History, like life, we have said, is never psychology in a vacuum. The psychic factors in history interact with the

C   51

other factors and are never found entirely out of relationship with them. If we are to have a genuinely interpretative history, merely supplementing purely positivist history by improvising psychological interpretations here and there will certainly not supply one.

It is at this point that we turn to the type of comparative, interpretative history which is associated with the name of Toynbee. The basic difficulty here is that Toynbee himself fails to give us a very coherent or satisfactory account of what he is trying to do, so that it is not surprising if many of his critics also fail to grasp the essential principle of his methodology. Some of them, for example, liken him to other writers with whom, despite superficial resemblances, he has almost nothing in common.

For example, he is often likened to Spengler. It will be said, of course, by such critics that as a student of history understood in a purely positivistic sense he is vastly superior to Spengler, but that his method is nevertheless similar and must ultimately fall under the same condemnation, even though that harsh judgement must in his case be qualified by a certain number of judicious compliments which Spengler's *Decline of the West* hardly deserves. Now it would seem that Toynbee's method differs basically from Spengler's. Spengler begins with an analogy which dominates his system of historical interpretation, as a kind of *a priori* judgement characteristic of his entire philosophy, the alleged analogy between historical and biological processes. Like biological processes, according to Spengler, the history of any particular society passes through stages of birth, growth, maturity, decay, and death. Thus Spengler approaches history with a preconceived pattern, not derived from the study of history, which he proceeds to impose, often ruthlessly, upon history. Toynbee, on the other hand, indulges in no analogy between historical and non-historical processes. He is concerned only with analogies, with recurrent patterns to be found in the course of history itself. It is no part of his purpose to reduce history to a species of non-history.

Marx also, like Spengler, begins his work on the basis of a judgement which reduces history to a kind of dramatic analogue of something which is in itself both non-dramatic and non-historical. For him the course of history is basically identical with and analogous to the laws of dialectic formulated in Hegel's *Logic*. In Marx's version of this dialectic, all history is the history of class struggles, and the class struggle always moves from thesis through antithesis to synthesis. Similar motifs can be found in Comte and many other expositors of the conventional philosophy of history. In all such writers, history ceases to be something *sui generis* and becomes simply a new version of non-historical patterns and themes transposed into a historical, dramatic medium. In all these cases the truth about history is not found by studying history but rather by studying something else and forcing non-historical patterns and interpretations upon the historical data.

It is small wonder that so many researching historians are chronically suspicious of what they call the philosophy of history, and quick to condemn Toynbee when they find him, as they suppose, doing very much the same kind of thing. Now it is undeniable that Toynbee does at times use language which invites this error of judgement. Thus he occasionally speaks of discovering 'laws of history,' perhaps analogous to the so-called scientific laws with which we interpret the cosmos, and we may very well be sceptical as to whether there are any laws of history, or of nature for that matter, quite of this kind. Again, he often describes himself as an empiricist—we have already seen how ambiguous the term empirical is—and he does not always make it clear that he is empirical only in the sense of seeking empirical verification for his formulae. But since history does not permit of experimental work in a

laboratory, this kind of verification must always be difficult to supply. Certainly, however, Toynbee does not
begin with any analogy between all history on the one
hand and some non-historical process on the other.
Rather he begins with a concentration upon history which
rather reminds us of the philosophical method of the
German philosopher Husserl and the phenomenological
school. We seem to hear him saying to himself, 'Let history
declare itself, let us so concentrate upon the data of history
that at last history itself speaks and manifests its own native
character.'

Of course, events never repeat themselves. Everything,
every event, is what it is and not anything else. Everything, every event, is unique. Yet this need not plunge
us into some kind of philosophical nominalism. Although
things and events never recur, patterns of relationship
between them do recur. We may detect in Toynbee a
kind of historical Platonism. Toynbee has that famous
'plastic eye' of Plato which can see at the same time both
the ultimate and basic particularity of the particular, and
the universality latent and undeclared in its situation. To
understand and to grasp the historical process is to see all
historical events as a vast, perhaps an infinite, number of
variations, infinitely varied and subtle variations, upon a
much smaller number, although still a very large one, of
persistent, recurrent patterns and themes which may be
described as inherent in history or chronic to history.
Every kind of rational knowledge has its own way of
dealing with this state of affairs. The absolute particularity of the particular must be acknowledged, and yet
everywhere this all pervading particularity is informed by
intelligible universals. Thus in medical science, A's smallpox really is distinct from B's smallpox, yet they are both
smallpox, and it is possible to write a scientific treatise on
smallpox in general which abstracts from all particular
instances of this unhappy phenomenon. The mind must

grasp both the particularity of the instances and the universality of the pattern at the same time. Again, in literary studies of some one particular author certain patterns persist which may be regarded as peculiarly characteristic of this particular writer. For example, all the plays of Ibsen are separate and distinct plays, yet undeniably one of them does again and again remind us of several others. Thus there is the theme of the cruelty of doctrinaire moral idealism which recurs in plays so distinct from each other as *Brand* and *The Wild Duck*. Poets may often be characterized by the recurrence in their work of certain archetypal images, and many of our best literary studies concentrate upon revealing data of this kind. In music, W. J. Turner has pointed out certain patterns which continually recur in Beethoven's slow movements. Each of these movements is distinct from any other, and yet each of them has a pattern which may be described as chronic to Beethoven, whether we find them in symphonies, concertos, or chamber music. Similar characteristics are discovered by experts in the realms of the plastic and visual arts.

Certainly the type of biblical interpretation which I have described as typological is platonic in this very general sense. Elijah in the cave is a very different episode from Jesus on the Cross, yet Elijah can say of himself something which was in his case an exaggeration but which Jesus on the Cross could have said of himself quite truly, 'Even I only am left, and they seek my life to take it away.'[1] The particularity is there and must be acknowledged, but so also, without in any way destroying the particularity, is the persistence and universality of the pattern.

In Toynbee's history, as in patristic biblical interpretation, particular events characterized by some one recurrent pattern are regarded as typical of each other. We

[1] 1 Kings 19. 10.

55

may speak of one as foreshadowing the other, and of the other as fulfilling the one. Such events may be grouped together and interpreted as one intelligible species of events. Thus, for example, Napoleon's invasion of Russia and Hitler's later invasion of Russia both evince one of these persistent patterns. The point is not that in each case it was Russia that was invaded—that is mere superficial resemblance and not genuine analogy at all—but because they both manifest and illustrate the recurrent historical theme which Toynbee calls 'the nemesis of militarism.' In order to make his conquests safe, the conqueror is always compelled to venture upon further aggressions until at last he conquers more than he can conceivably defend. His resources are exhausted in conquest, and to defend what he has conquered becomes an impossible task. Sometimes this process will manifest itself in a single lifetime, as in the cases of Hitler and Napoleon; at other times it will take up the much longer period of a lasting political regime like the Roman Empire, but again and again the same pattern confronts us in history: a career of ambitious and imposing conquest always ends in the necessity of engaging in a new defensive action. There is no question here of any recurrent event. Hitler was not Napoleon and it would be grossly unfair to Napoleon to stress any kind of personal resemblance. Yet the patterns are undeniably analogous. Even at the very height of Hitler's triumphs it was always possible for hope to feed and sustain itself by reflecting on the fate of Napoleon. The one foreshadowed and was fulfilled by the other.

The interpretation of history from this point of view depends on our capacity so to employ this comparative, analogical method as to grasp these persistent historical patterns, to group them together and interpret them as an intelligible species, so that at last we can say that even though we remain as ignorant as we were before about what in fact will happen in the future, at least we know what the themes of history are and what they will continue to be. This kind of historical interpretation cannot of itself reconstruct historical events; certainly it cannot enable us to foresee the future; but it can tell us what history is about, enable us to interpret it as an intelligible drama, pressing upon our attention certain persistent themes of life and destiny. This is a point of view which enables the theologian to interpret all human history as a kind of Bible, and it supplies him with a concept of historical thought which is analogous to and continuous with the kind of biblical interpretation on which the classical theological thought of the Christian Church is based.

In the history of Christian thought, theological reason manifests itself as a kind of intermediary between philosophical reason on the one hand and historical reason on the other. Christian theology begins as an interpretation of history and culminates in an interpretation of being and destiny. It has in common with the history the necessity and discipline of interpreting a particular block of data, a particular series of historical reports and facts. It has in common with philosophy an absorbing interest in vast problems of ultimate and universal being and destiny. What the theologian has in common with the philosopher distinguishes him from the historian, and what he has in common with the historian distinguishes him from the philosopher. This may mean that his work scandalizes both historians and philosophers. But if they are more discerning and understanding of the wholeness of intellectual endeavour they will see in the theologian a kind of missing link in a chain of coherence, a clue enabling each to discover his underlying affinity with the other.

But to say this may be dangerously to misinterpret certain particular features of the contemporary situation. The kind of historiography with which Christian theology has such close affinity is not so much the merely critical evidence-seeking historiography of the nineteenth-century historians, of which classical theology for the most part knew nothing, because it had not yet been born, but rather the interpretative, typological historiography which we find in the Bible and in early Christian biblical interpretation, and which has experienced a kind of twentieth-century resurrection in Toynbee's *A Study of History*. I have been concerned so much with Toynbee's work in this book precisely because this is the kind of history with which Christian theology has most in common.

Of course, it would be absurd to suppose that Toynbee is in any sense inerrant, or that we can possibly accept his results and teachings as they stand. I am not defending the Toynbean conclusions but rather commending the Toynbean method. I have before me a volume of critical essays and reviews of Toynbee's *A Study of History* edited by Mr. Ashley Montague and entitled *Toynbee and History*,[1] side by side with the final volume of *A Study of History: Reconsiderations*.[2] They make fascinating reading. The distinguished critics never perceive at any point what I regard as the most important of Toynbee's affinities, that is, with the typological interpreters of scripture in the early Church. Some of them merely point out that Toynbee was badly mistaken about the character of certain historical events falling within the area of their own specialized knowledge. This, after all, was only to be expected. Many of them are very critical of Toynbee's claim to be an empiricist. But always these writers fail to perceive the ambiguity of the term empirical, and do little more than imply that Toynbee fails to be empirical in the sense which they would give to that term—usually a more or less eighteenth-century sense, and almost always a positivist and phenomenological one.

[1] Porter Sargent. Boston, 1956.   [2] Oxford University Press, 1961.

By far the best criticism of Toynbee in *Toynbee and History*, as it seems to me, is contributed by Pitirim A. Sorokin. He points out very tellingly that what Toynbee calls a civilization is not a real system of interdependent parts but 'mere conglomerations of various civilized objects and phenomena united only by special adjacency but not by causal or meaningful bonds.'[1] They are not 'real species of society; they can hardly be treated as unities, and can hardly have any uniformities in their genesis, growth and decline.' This seems to me not entirely true of any civilization or culture pattern. We can always find many important elements which compose an interdependent system of culture. On the other hand, it is undeniable that any civilization will contain many apparently accidental elements which seem to be there in fact, without there being any reason for their presence. While I doubt whether any civilization is, in fact, a merely accidental congeries of irrelevant adjacencies, every civilization will include accidental material of this kind. Indeed, Toynbee has at least one concept which would help us to explain these facts: the concept of the internal proletariat. Every civilization known to history includes a vast number of members who are physically within the area of the civilization, who are essential to it because they work for it, but who spiritually do not belong to it, who do not participate in at all events its higher values. They belong to its body but not to its spirit. They are part of it materially, but not part of it metaphysically.

This is perhaps one reason why some species of materialism has seemed to some people the proper democratic philosophy. Only if we look upon a civilization as a material process producing material goods for material enjoyment can we hold that a civilization is the kind of thing in which all its members at the same time can fully

[1] *Toynbee and History*, p. 180.

59

participate. For example, we speak of Western civilization, and no doubt in using the phrase we have in mind its literature, its art, its religious and philosophical ideas, its sciences and political forms, the purposes which its technology is supposed at least in theory to subserve, and so on. But what, we may ask, has the crowd at the football match, or on Saturday night in Times Square or Piccadilly, or the muttered comment at the strip-tease burlesque, got to do with civilization understood and interpreted in these exalted terms? And the answer must be that these things co-exist by accident rather than by immanent design. They are adjacent but they have no real relationship to each other.

Despite the exhortations to unity the fact is that our civilization is deeply divided right down the middle. Its values, created by a small minority and appreciated by a larger minority, entirely elude the minds of the vast majority. We have our internal proletariat to-day just as truly as the Roman Empire did. Are we to suppose that in Attic Greece everyone understood Socrates, or that in Elizabethan England the whole population venerated Shakespeare? It is certainly true that there has never been a system of civilization in any such highly integrated sense. I think this is an important criticism of Toynbee and yet, in a sense, Toynbee, with his concept of the internal proletariat, the spiritually disinherited men, knew it all the time.

The same thing is true in Church history. All the members of the Church, of course, are in a very real sense *in* the Church, but by no means all of them are in an equally profound sense *of* the Church. It is always possible for many of us not to know of what spirit we are. Indeed, this fact presents the parish priest, the preacher, and the pastor, with his gravest problem and challenge, and, transposed into political terms, it is also the gravest problem and challenge confronting democracy. How can we bring about a situation in which the people who are with us physically can also be with us mentally and spiritually? Is education the solution? It will have to be a very different and much more successful kind of education than anything with which we are now acquainted. Or perhaps Toynbee is right, and there is no solution. There never will be a civilization without an internal proletariat, for the internal proletariat is one of the persistent patterns and themes of historical process. For any civilization, of course, the gravest danger is some possible coalition of the internal with the external proletariat, the people outside who do not belong making common cause with the people inside who do not belong. There is certainly no sign in a contemporary history that we have moved or grown and progressed to a point at which this chronic historical theme begins to disappear, and to observe that this is so is one more way of verifying the basic thesis of Toynbee.

We do not know what will happen, but we do know that history will continue to be history. We can know what history is *about*. The future contains variations of undreamed of novelty. All that we know is what the themes are which will be varied. We do not know what will happen, we do not know what the future course of history will unfold, but we do know that the history which is to come will be of one piece with the history which is past, the whole composing a unity, in a sense non-repetitive, and yet in another sense having a cumulative effect, so that the element of repetition in no ways dulls our expectancy that all will move at last to some ultimate, majestic conclusion which no doubt will seem predestined and fated once we know what it is, although strangely enough it could never have been predicted by those who knew only what went before.

Man in history may perhaps remind us of Coleridge's *Ancient Mariner*. 'In his loneliness and fixedness he yearneth towards the journeying Moon, and the stars that still sojourn, yet still move onward; and everywhere the blue sky belongs to them, and is their appointed rest, and their native country and their own natural homes, which they enter unannounced as lords that are certainly expected, and yet there is a silent joy at their arrival.'[1]

[1] Author's note accompanying Part IV, lines 236-71.

CHAPTER 3

THE PHILOSOPHY OF HISTORY AND THE PHILOSOPHY OF RELIGION

SO far, we have claimed in effect that the typological method of interpretation is the proper one to use when what we are searching for is clues to the meaning of the process under investigation. We note the persistences and recurrences, the strikingly important analogies between various groups of events, and in such a way we become aware of the basic themes which are, so to speak, chronic to and at stake in history, and which provide it with its abiding substance and subject matter. We may remark that this is always the way in which meaning is perceived, not only in history, but also in literature and art. Again, it is the way in which a child gradually learns his own mother tongue. Words and patterns of words constantly recur and so, through familiarity, exercise a meaningful impact upon one beginning to hear and use them.

I have defended the Toynbean method without attempting to say anything that would identify me in any way with the Toynbean results, the actual concepts and doctrines which emerge from his use of his method. Now it is important to consider the general effect of these concepts and doctrines because, although most of the critics of Toynbee have, in fact, concentrated on attacking his method, it is impossible to resist the strong impression that the reason why so many contemporary historians dislike Toynbee is not so much the methods he employs as the general tone, drift, and substance of his results. Inevitably, Toynbee seems a reactionary thinker to all those who regard the radical secularization of modern history, philosophy, and science as a promising and progressive development. And, of course, there is a sense in which Toynbee may rightly be described as reactionary.

A Study of History is surely the best thing of its kind that has appeared since St. Augustine's *City of God*. Indeed, the fifteen centuries that intervene between the publication of these two great works contain remarkably little fit to be compared with either. These two vast books belong together to such a degree that it is almost impossible to discuss one without referring to the other. In *The City of God* St. Augustine attempted to provide a biblical and theological analysis of world history. Of course, the amount of world history which St. Augustine had at his command was small when compared with the range of Toynbee's historical knowledge. But it was sufficient, wedded to the extraordinary breadth of view and philosophical and theological penetration of St. Augustine, to yield highly significant results, and the fact that Toynbee in the twentieth century, when much more modern history has occurred and much more ancient history is known than in St. Augustine's time, can still come substantially to the same conclusions is, to say the least, highly significant. St. Augustine's problem arose from the sharp contrast between classical views of history as a repetitive cyclic process and the biblical view of history as something that begins with a determinate event, the creation, proceeds through another determinate event, the Incarnation or Fullness of Time, to a third determinate event, the end of the world and the establishment of the Kingdom of God. For St. Augustine the intermediate event, the Incarnation, is analogous to the creation, because Christ is the new creature, and analogous to the final consummation of all things because Christ is the eschatological creature or 'last thing.' He is the last or ultimate event occurring by a strange paradox in the middle of history, so that the last or ultimate event is at the same time both he central and the primordial event, through whom the worlds were made, through whom the world is redeemed, and through whom the end of all things is consummated.

Now, of course, many Christian thinkers have dealt with this clash between the classical and the biblical view of history simply by repudiating the classical view as altogether untrue, and strongly reaffirming the biblical view. St. Augustine, however, is more subtle, and more appreciative of the insights of the classical mind. He sees history not as one single integral process, but rather as the intertwining of two quite distinct processes. For St. Augustine, history may be described as 'a tale of two cities.' He distinguishes the City of Man or, as we may call it, secular, temporal history, from the City of God, or sacred, religious, and spiritual history. In his view, secular history is adequately described in a more or less cyclic way. It is a going round and round, which either gets nowhere at all, or at best, gets somewhere only because it is used as an instrumentality by sacred history. Secular history goes round and round, but sacred history goes on and on. In the actual course of events the relationship between the two is intimate, complex and subtle, but always it is true that secular history is the means by which, with which, and through which, sacred history moves ever forward. From this point of view, religious and spiritual development is the business end of history. It is that element in history which really counts and ultimately prevails. Secular history, as the very name implies, belongs merely to time and cannot escape or rise above its temporal limitations. He who lives by time must die by time. Sacred history, on the other hand, is a subtle blend of eternity and time, eternity temporizing, but never quite eternity temporized.

Toynbee expresses the same point of view in a daring simile which occurs in his book of essays *Civilization on Trial*.[1] He compares the course of history to a boy riding

[1] Oxford University Press, London, 1948.

a bicycle. The wheels go round and round while the boy goes on and on. The wheels represent secular history, the boy sacred history. Perhaps no passage in the vast corpus of Toynbee's writings makes quite so clear his fundamental agreement with St. Augustine.

But in the modern world, at least from the eighteenth century onwards, men have almost unanimously abandoned this Augustinian view of history. The essence of the doctrine of progress as first announced in the eighteenth century by the French Abbé Bernardin de St. Pierre is a transferring of the attributes of Augustine's sacred history to our secular history. Now it is secular history that goes on and on and sacred history that either goes round and round or even sometimes supinely stays where it is. For eighteenth- and nineteenth-century secular thinkers religion is a kind of epiphenomenon which makes no real difference to and plays no real part in the course of history. It is set on one side as a mere turning away from history, a kind of obsession with eternity, equated with mere passivity or stability, which wastefully consumes human energy and creative power, without producing any concrete result. Either that, or religiosity is itself a phase of secular history which progresses side by side and in harmony with the other phases. In either case the two-city version of history is in effect abandoned. It becomes, according to the doctrine of progress, a tale of one city with the body of secular history interpreted as though it were in fact the soul of sacred history.

Perhaps that is why modern history since the eighteenth century is so very much a tale of political fanaticism and intolerance, just as the previous centuries had been scarred by sporadic outbursts of religious fanaticism and intolerance. Historical epochs can be understood and distinguished from each other in terms of what ordinary people of limited insight and understanding are willing to get excited about. The modern secular political fanaticism and intolerance is just as ugly and lethal as the earlier religious fanaticism and intolerance, perhaps indeed more so. Regarded simply as instances of fanaticism and intolerance, there is nothing to choose between them. Yet we can say, from the point of view of St. Augustine and Toynbee, that the religious fanatics and persecutors, however gravely sinful and misled, were, in fact, excited about profounder and deeper themes. There is a sense in which a man could undergo a profounder and more valid martyrdom in a Spanish *Auto da Fe* than in Dachau, Belsen, Auschwitz, or Siberia. There is a difference between dying for something that matters infinitely and eternally, and being murdered for the sake of something that matters very much but only for the moment, though we must beware of pressing this distinction too far, for that which matters eternally and infinitely has an odd habit of somehow incarnating itself in that which matters very much and for the moment. We must make the distinction between the two, but not too absolutely or fundamentally. The temporal is not the eternal, but the temporal is no more irrelevant to the eternal than the eternal is irrevelant to the temporal.

It is true, however, to say that the doctrine of progress as received and formulated in the eighteenth and nineteenth centuries is a secularization of the doctrine of providence, a decking out of the profane in the etherial robes of the sacred. Under such conditions more and more people have lost any sense of the sacred and totally misconceived and misinterpreted the profane. It must always be so. Where it is no longer possible to make any valid distinctions the intellect is plunged into a kind of pseudo-mystical fog. We never see anything clearly except when we see it against the background of something else. If we cannot distinguish the City of Man from the City of God we cannot really even distinguish the City of Man. So we become secular about our religion and religious about our secularity. Nothing is clearly seen because nothing is clearly distinguished from anything else. The mere pious distinction between truth and falsehood is not enough. What really matters is the distinction between truth and truth.

In the twentieth century, of course, we have become sceptical even about the doctrine of progress, and this means that most people are left without any category for interpreting history at all, except perhaps those psychological categories which we have already examined and found wanting. For human history, as we have seen, is emphatically not a process in which psychic factors exercise a sovereign sway. In this situation some people try to rescue a sort of vestigial doctrine of progress by pointing to factors which do seem, at all events during relatively short periods of history, and especially during our own, to show signs of some sort of progressive and cumulative capacity. For example, there is the progress of knowledge, and especially of science, and the rapid development of technology. If other things do not seem to progress very much, at all events during our own present patch of history, these things at least seem to be developing very rapidly. In this way we can move back to something that faintly recalls the Augustinian doctrine. Most things in life go round and round, but science and technology go on and on. The endlessly repetitious world of commonplace human affairs is contrasted with the rapidly developing world of the scientist and the engineer. We must beware, however, of making too much of this. The same phenomenon has been noted before and interpreted very differently with perhaps rather profounder philosophical insight. Thus Toynbee points out that during the last phases of the Roman Empire there was considerable technical progress which did nothing to save it. Lucretius noted that the technical progress of his time was taking people into deeper and deeper waters, making possible greater and greater catastrophies, from which they had less and less chance of saving themselves. The whole passage has a very modern ring.

More recently Spengler has interpreted the immense technical progress of America as a sign of the old age of our western civilization. It is old men and not young ones who are most of all interested in devices which secure ease and comfort and save labour and effort. For Spengler, America is above all the old age of the West, that phase of western history which most of all suggests its approaching decline and demise. For him the glory of youth and creativity is over so far as the West is concerned. The age of Shakespeare and Leonardo da Vinci, the age of genius, the zenith of creative power, is done with, and now nothing awaits us but more Edisons, and the scientific medical research which aims at keeping an ageing people alive in some kind of painless comfort a little longer. Of course, in so far as all this is true it implies that even the temper of our scientific and technical progress will soon begin to decelerate, that it belongs to our own patch of history, a patch of history which is drawing towards its close. I am not, in any way, accepting these verdicts, but simply remarking that they would appear to cast some doubt on any merely scientific and technological concept of progress.

Another way out of this impasse is, like Toynbee, to execute an intellectual manoeuvre which, to the modern mind, by which I really mean the eighteenth-century mind surviving through the nineteenth century, appears to be reactionary. St. Augustine was right after all, and the eighteenth century was wrong to transpose his categories. It is useless to deck secular history with the attributes of sacred history. The garments will not fit, and we must not be surprised if they are beginning to fall off. They were always much too big. The basic theme of human history is a religious theme, because that too is the basic theme of human existence. The story of the irreligious man is primarily the tragic story of what he denies. The story of the man who is merely sceptical and indifferent is the apathetic story of what he ignores. In both cases it is fundamentally a religious story. Of the one man we must say that he could not love the highest when he saw it, of the other that he could not see the highest when it loved him. Human existence in history is a religious process and must be understood and interpreted in religious and theological categories. Religious history goes on and on because, although temporal in its substance, it is eternal in its vision. Secular history remains incapsulated in mere temporality.

But if Toynbee's view of history seems Augustinian and reactionary to many contemporary historians whose point of view is dominated by a secularistic bias derived from the eighteenth century, his view of religion seems equally reactionary and unsatisfactory to many contemporary theologians. We may say that Toynbee's religious views, as expressed, for example, in his book *An Historian's Approach to Religion*,[1] is very largely a nineteenth-century one, replete with overtones from idealistic philosophy and based on the outlook of the old-fashioned comparative religion and philosophy of religion school. Religion, from this point of view, is essentially a sacred teaching based on the kind of philosophical insight characteristic of devout and insightful religious teachers with their profound ethical and mystical sensitivity. There have been, of course, many of these religious teachers who have flourished at many different times and many different places, but basically their point of view converges upon certain central types of belief which it is the task of a genuine religious philosophy to outline and defend. The basic unity of all the teachings of the higher religions is demonstrated by an intellectual discipline usually entitled

[1] Oxford University Press, London, 1956.

70

Comparative Religion, and the truth of this interpretation of religion, discovered by the careful analysis, comparison and interpretation of the so-called higher religions, is supposed to be demonstrated by another, more speculative discipline entitled the *Philosophy of Religion*. The result is a belief in religion in general which is not a belief in any religion in particular, and this is a point of view very different from that of the Bible and the biblical theologians. Indeed, it is no exaggeration to say that the Bible and the biblical theologians do not really believe in religion at all. The normal name for religion in the Bible is idolatry, and it is always strongly and sternly contrasted with the revealed religion which culminates in the Incarnation. Revealed religion, we may say, is rooted in history and in particular historical experiences, whereas religion in general represents a kind of flight from history to the eternal on the part of devout, contemplative and mystical minds.

This does not imply that religion as such is insignificant or unimportant to the biblical theologian. For him religion is a man-made thing, whereas revealed religion is a God-made thing, but the man-made thing is nevertheless significant because in man and human culture it creates a special kind of context in which God can appear, develops a peculiar form of human sensitivity to which God can speak. Thus religion may be important and even precious, however defective and desperately in need of redemption. From this point of view the biblical theologian may say that Christianity is not a religion at all. He would prefer to define it not as *a* religion but as *the* redemption of religion. This at least implies that religion is a reality well worth redeeming, though he may very well add that nothing is quite so hard to redeem.

In one respect this Christian and biblical distinction between religion in general and revealed religion has a positive advantage over the religiosity of the nineteenth-century comparative religion school. The emphatic distinction between religion in general and revealed religion at least enables us to avoid the questionable and possibly unjust contrast between the so-called *higher* religions and the supposedly *lower* religions so characteristic of the teachings of the comparative religionists. It is most important in dealing with the whole area of religion to find a way of doing justice to the lower religions, and this is something which the biblical approach to the problems of comparative religion does perhaps succeed in doing. The mere distinction between the higher religions and the others ignores two things: first, the real value of the kinds of religion written off by implication as lower religions, and, secondly, the importance of the distinction between revealed religion and refined and sophisticated religiosity. The true distinction is not that between higher and lower religion, but that between superstition, mythology, and revealed religion.

Superstition is the belief that by the use of certain techniques, mainly magical, it is possible for man to master certain spiritual powers and use them in the service of his own purposes. In the cruder forms of superstition these human wants and purposes are for the most part of a merely physical variety. Thus agricultural peoples need rain and resort to magical rain-making ceremonies; there are similar ceremonials which are supposed to produce a climate and attitude favourable to success in child-bearing, fishing, hunting, and war. Even in contemporary sectarian Christianity there is a good deal of talk about the supposed power of prayer which vests it with some similarly magical attributes, and at the same time, unfortunately, renders impossible any genuinely Christian understanding of prayer.

Frazer used to distinguish absolutely between magic and religion, and to affiliate magic to modern science and technology rather than to religion. Of course, it was always possible to reply that this fundamental distinction between religion and magic is a distinction that almost all primitive religions completely ignore. The incompatibility of religion and magic was not observed by primitive man. But that does not necessarily imply that the distinction is altogether useless. Certainly both primitive magic and modern scientific technology are dominated by the idea of man appropriating, mastering, and using certain powers in the service of his own purposes. Religion, on the other hand, always seems to be a human acknowledgement of man's dependence upon a Power which he cannot master, so that now, from this religious standpoint, it is man who must be mastered, and used in the service of that Power, rather than the other way round. The mere fact that so much primitive religion fails to take note of the distinction between magic and religion does not necessarily invalidate it.

There is, however, a sophisticated form of magical superstition still very much alive even at the present time which heavily reinforces this distinction. Sophisticated superstition attempts to utilize spiritual power by religious practice, not in the service of man's more physical purposes, but certainly in the service of his psychological and spiritual objectives. Religion may be thought of as a kind of psychological hygiene, a set of practices which induce in men desirable mental and spiritual attitudes and states of being. Thus many people value religious practice because it is supposed to produce a condition called 'peace of mind,' while others speak of the comfort which is supposed to be its human by-product. Others value religion because of its alleged capacity to produce desirable ethical consequences, or even important social consequences like social stability and creativity. Thus in some quarters we may be told that the nation was greater and more energetic when men read their Bibles and attended church more frequently than they do now, with the suggestion that a revival of religious fervour on a national scale would produce, as a kind of by-product, a revival of national glory. In Hinayana Buddhism religious practice is supposed to produce a kind of majestic indifference to the vicissitudes of life, to take the devout man so far beyond the desires centred in his selfhood that life and time and history lose their power to inflict pain upon him with their sharp and disappointing stings. Religion, from this point of view, makes a man indifferent to the harshness of his temporal fate, and then ushers him into a world of invincible serenity, beyond all desire, ambition, and hope. The resemblance of religion so conceived and evaluated to certain kinds of psychiatric technique is very remarkable, and no doubt all this may be described as white magic, but magical it remains. By contrast with the cruder magic of the rain-making ceremonies, for example, the consequences that are supposed to ensue upon religious practice appear to be more spiritual, but human purposes remain in the centre of the picture as man thus sees in religion a power to act desirably upon himself.

Perhaps we should prefer the word 'psychic' to the word 'spiritual' in this context. The word 'spiritual' is very difficult to define. For most people the spiritual is the non-material, so that for them the psychic and ideal is spiritual. Spiritual purposes are any purposes that are non-physical and non-economic. But from the point of view of biblical theology too much has been made of this misleading dichotomy between matter and spirit. The distinction between the personal and the impersonal is a vastly superior one, much more to our purpose, when we are trying to understand the meaning of the distinction between the spiritual and the non-spiritual, and it is this distinction which so many of the so-called higher religions have found it difficult to comprehend. In the far east, in particular, we find widespread what has been called the cult of the impersonal sacred, in a way that rather fails to see that there is really very little difference between an impersonal sacred and an impersonal profane. For those of us who stand in the biblical tradition personality is incomparably the best thing that reality contains, and where we cannot trace personality we cannot recognize any high form of value. For us the spiritual is the personal. Personality is the phenomenal word which discerns and traces the outlines of the spiritual. Spirituality is the metaphysical term which evaluates personality and awards it the supreme position in the scale of being. In any religion in which personality is denied the highest place the biblical mind discerns some species of magic, however refined and sophisticated and concealed. From this point of view many of the so-called higher religions, particularly those characteristic of the far east, differ less from gross superstition than would at first sight appear. They have failed to understand that genuine spirituality always puts personality in the highest possible place.

From superstition we turn to mythology. Whether we look at Hinduism and Buddhism or at ancient Greece, the general tendency of merely religious development is to turn from mythology to some kind of religious philosophy. Neither in India nor in Greece is the mythology actively denied, rather it is overlaid by more sophisticated, philosophical elements which propose to interpret, and somehow, in interpreting, appear to explode the myths. Biblical religion takes a higher view of mythology because mythology at least insists on interpreting reality in personal terms. Of course, the term mythology is difficult to define. A great deal of mythology is simply concerned with what may be called prehistory, early phases of human existence which have left us with no detailed and specific records of any kind, although they may to some extent be explored by archaeology and ethnology. The value of mythology in relation to prehistory is its strong affirmation that human events of which the historian can know nothing have nevertheless one essential characteristic in common with the events about which the historian can know a great deal, i.e., they were and must have been personal events. When dealing conjecturally with the events of prehistory we tend inevitably to drop into impersonal process language, to talk, for example, about the results of the desiccation of the soil in the once fertile middle east, quite forgetting that what must have occurred was a series of human personal reactions to these catastrophies.

Toynbee's insight is of great value in relation to this distinction between impersonal process and personal drama or event. For him a geological change like the desiccation of the soil of the fertile middle east, which from the naturalistic point of view we should call a geological process, is at the same time, from the human and historical point of view, a menacing challenge. The human response to such a challenge cannot be recorded or understood in impersonal process language, nor is it in any sense a necessary or inevitable response. In fact, different groups of people respond to the same challenge in different ways. For example, in the case of the pre-historic desiccation of the fertile soil of the middle east, no doubt many of the primitive food gatherers who had lived easily in this delightful Garden of Eden failed to make any response at all, and merely died of malnutrition and starvation. Others migrated southward into Africa, pushing on until they found conditions not unlike those to which they had been accustomed. Others again remained where they were, and made a creative response to the challenge by inventing a system of agriculture based upon the irrigation of the soil through the capture and retention of the flood waters from the great rivers of the middle east which were released at the time of their annual inundations. According to Toynbee, it is in such

76

creative responses to menacing challenge that new civilizations are born. The challenge itself may sometimes, although by no means always, be an impersonal process, but the response is always a dramatic personal act, and the response is always an option, never a necessity. Thus, when lack of sufficient evidence prevents us from giving any account of such an event in the ordinary language of history, we shall be nearer the truth if we employ the language of mythology—as in the familiar Garden of Eden story—than we should be if we merely relaxed into impersonal process language.

Even when mythology deals with more metaphysical things, like the creation of the world and the origin of the human race—which we might call pre-history B to distinguish it from pre-history A—it still insists on telling us a story, using personal and dramatic language. It never merely analyses an impersonal process but insists on interpreting all things in its category of drama.

Nowadays, however, we have the strong tendency to use the word myth in relation to any belief once widely entertained which we no longer credit. Thus Bultmann appears to use the word 'myth' to describe many ideas which are not properly speaking mythological at all. For example, the kind of cosmology which we find taken for granted in the Bible, with a flat earth and the dome of the heavens spread above it and the mirky hellish depths beneath, is, after all, not a myth but rather a kind of early science. It is an interpretation of the cosmos based simply upon an uncritical acceptance and interpretation of sense data, a kind of pure, unsophisticated empiricism. This is what physical reality looks like to primitive man. For that matter, this is what physical reality actually looks like to modern man. It is no more mythological than phlogiston, or the now discarded theory of the fixity of species.

Bultmann, of course, wishes to interpret what he calls mythology rather than merely to reject it, but somehow

77

or other once his interpretations have been accepted, the myths themselves seem to diminish in importance, and Christian belief begins more and more to be expressed in merely philosophical language. Thus I quote from his *History and Eschatology*: 'Christian faith believes that man does not have the freedom which is presupposed for historical decisions.'[1] Now we may very well ask ourselves whether 'Christian faith' ever believes anything of the kind. Christian faith believes that Christ, the eternal Son of God, the second Person of the Holy Trinity, was born as Jesus, as a man among men, suffered under Pontius Pilate, was crucified, dead and buried, rose again the third day, and so on. Now, a Christian philosopher may very well say, in the course of his interpretation of what Christian faith does believe in, that all this may indeed imply that man 'does not have the freedom which is presupposed for historical decisions.' But Christian faith, properly speaking, is the faith in the reality and power of the events themselves, not a faith in some philosopher's gloss upon them.

Of course, Christian faith differs from mythological faith by its insistence that this unique Christian myth is not myth at all but history, yet in other respects it is, indeed, very close to the spirit of mythology. Like mythology, it first proclaims events and then adds an interpretation of them which it honestly feels is the only one they can possibly bear. Thus Christianity, although distinguished from all mythology by its insistence that in the long run we must pass from mythology to history, nevertheless has a great deal in common with mythology, and I think must deliberately prefer mythological paganism to the more philosophically inclined higher religions of the far east, and this even on philosophical grounds.

[1] 'History and Eschatology.' *The Gifford Lectures*, 1955. University of Edinburgh Press, 1957, p. 150.

At least pagan mythology has a surer grasp of the supremacy of personality than philosophical and metaphysical cults of an impersonal sacred. Mythological religion does not rest upon history as biblical religion does, but it is at least continuous with history, and thus has more in common with the kind of religion which does rest upon history. The kind of comparative religion which makes much of distinctions between higher and lower religion is unjust to the insights of mythology, but a biblical and Christian study of the same data would award them a much higher place. Certainly the ultimate context of biblical religion is mythological. In the Bible there is no suggestion of anything remotely like a religious-philosophical cult of an impersonal sacred. Where events are historically unknown they are mythologically imagined, and the mythological fiction must always be nearer the truth than the apathetical philosophical formula, because at least it weaves its fictions in terms of persons and events.

Nevertheless, from the standpoint of revealed religion mythology is not enough. Only genuine history can really reveal the God who is lord of history. And this, of course, implies that all positive revealing events have their *where* and their *when*, that scandal of particularity which so puzzles and confounds the mere religious philosopher.

Religious truth is a kind of universal truth, for nothing can be true religiously which is not true universally. To some modern thinkers this has seemed to imply that no religious truth can have any peculiar relationship to a particular event occupying a particular place in space and time. In the eighteenth century Lessing declared that 'accidental historical truths can never serve as proofs for eternal truths of the reason; and that the transition by which it is proposed to base an eternal truth upon historical testimony is a leap.'[1] Of course, here we are discussing the revelation rather than the proof of an

[1] *Ueber den Beweis des Geistes und der Kraft.* Vol. X.

eternal truth, which is not quite the same thing, but with this qualification Lessing's dictum does not differ significantly from the view of a contemporary philosopher like Jaspers, who is of interest to us precisely because his religious ideas so strongly resemble Toynbee's. I usually find myself in close agreement with Jaspers, but his attitude towards Hebrew ideas of revelation betrays a certain intellectual anti-semitism. 'The belief,' he writes, 'that God manifests Himself at a given place and time, that He has revealed Himself directly at one place in time . . . makes God appear as a fixed thing, an object in the world.'[1] Jaspers thus succeeds in being religious in a philosophical way without for one moment deferring to the claims of any particular religion. God is the universal, timeless truth and therefore cannot achieve a genuine relationship with the kind of reality which we enjoy in space and time. God is the universal and therefore any particular revelation with its *where* and its *when* is impossible.

But there is an ambiguity about the concept of the universal which is ignored when the contrast between the universal and the particular is too sharply drawn. Of course, the truth about God, whatever it may be, is universally true, true at all times and in all places, but because the truth about God is universal truth it does not follow that God himself is a kind of philosophical universal. God, in fact, is not a universal but a singular, the ultimate and absolute singular, and it is an error of logic to suppose that a singular is the same kind of thing as a universal. That philosophers, even religious philosophers, are so prone to make this mistake is due to the fact that the philosopher in his philosophical work is inevitably more concerned with the idea of God, and its role or place in some pet metaphysical or philosophical scheme, than with the reality of God. Now, of course, it is true that all the ideas of God which we entertain are ways of

[1] *Myth and Christianity*, The Noonday Press, New York, 1958, p. 41.

'confessing' that reality, and the means by which we render to our consciousness of that reality some sort of approximate intellectual justice. But the reality must always transcend the idea. This is why the religious man is urging a consideration vital to the health of philosophy when he reminds us that our primary duty towards God is not merely to think him, or to think in terms of him, but to worship him. Worship is a form of love, indeed, the highest form, and the most important characteristic of love is that it runs ahead of knowledge and embraces not merely what is known of the beloved, but both the known and the unknown in the unity in which they exist in the beloved himself. When we love, we love what we partly know and partly do not know, for love is always the love of the whole. The truth about God then is universally true, but God is not for that reason a universal.

Of course, even in Platonic philosophy the universal has its own distinctive kind of particularity. The Platonic universal is universal in relation to its appropriate range of particulars, but it is always this particular universal in relation to all other universals. Thus the notion of universality does not altogether exclude and is not the complete antithesis of the notion of particularity. Further, we must distinguish between the merely logical universals, arrived at by abstraction from particulars, the universal as the name of the common nature or structure which a wide variety of particulars share, and the idea of the concrete universal, which somehow includes the particularity of all its particulars. We may say that in those Platonic dialogues in which the universal is conceived in a logical fashion, the particulars are said to *imitate* the universal, whereas in those other Platonic dialogues which are moving towards a doctrine of the concrete universal, the particulars are said to *participate* in the universal, and in turn the universal participates in the particular. Thus God, at least from the moment of the creation, has a certain kind of particularity appropriate to his being. He is God and not anything that God has made, and this does confer upon him a certain kind of particularity *vis-à-vis* all the things that compose the creation.

Once we have grasped this it is very difficult to follow a philosopher like Jaspers when he tells us that there cannot be any particular revelation. The religious philosopher who denies the possibility of a direct and particular revelation is saying to us, in effect, 'If my idea of God is correct, then he cannot have such a relationship to space and time as would make a particular revelation possible.' But this is to claim for his own idea of God an absolute adequacy which such a philosopher would certainly not concede to anyone else's idea of God. This is to allow our idea of God to master the reality instead of humbly and gladly conceding that the reality must always transcend the idea. If God is truly free, then there is no possibility of any *a priori* denial that a particular revelation is one of the things that could conceivably happen if God so willed it. Any attempt to demonstrate that no such thing could conceivably happen really rests upon the prejudice according to which God never would will anything of the kind. But have we any reason to suppose that such a prejudice is valid, or, indeed, could we possibly have any reason for supposing it? It is all rather like those philosophers who tell us that, of course, God could work miracles in theory, but in practice would resolutely decline to do anything of the kind. Surely no one knows the private mind of God well enough to dogmatize in quite this way.

Toynbee takes a view of the higher religions fundamentally in line with Jasper's philosophical views, and with the conventional schools of comparative religion which have taught for several generations in our colleges and universities. The claim of any religion to be in any unique sense the revelation of God is repudiated as an idolization of particular religious institutions, and a kind of general religious truth about which the higher religions are supposed to be in agreement is substituted. We may say that according to Toynbee the higher religions share a valuable approximation to the truth about God, and a strong, healthy common conviction about the nature of religious existence, but that no one of them contains in any exclusive sense the reality of the divine presence or the push and pull of the divine initiative. God is never, not even for us men and for our salvation, either here or there. He is always imprisoned in his ineffable everywhere, and from this horrid incarceration he can never escape.

Thus we find in Toynbee the paradox of the historian who insists on taking a religious view of history while resolutely declining to take a historical view of religion. This, it seems to me, is the most important criticism of the Toynbean synthesis. The trouble about Toynbee is not so much that he is frequently wrong about this or that particular question of fact, nor even that he so often fails to use his own chosen method either correctly or convincingly. The real difficulty lies far deeper, the whole theory is somehow lop-sided, indeed, unilateral. Religion contributes much to our understanding of history, but the particular events of which history is composed inhabit a world of locality and restriction in space and time which is ultimately quite irrelevant to religion. God can be symbolized in terms of the events which compose the historical record, but he cannot really be in any of them. Such a God is an eternal, timeless God who cannot achieve any genuine accommodation with time.

We shall have to discuss the relationship between eternity and time in a later chapter. Here I will leave the matter for the moment, saying no more than this. If the eternity which God inhabits is mere non-time, then, of course, it follows that since God exists in eternity he cannot be in time, and no particular self-revealing activity under these conditions of all-prevailing particularity which dominate and govern time is thinkable. From this point of view the gulf between God and man is metaphysical, and neither God nor man can cross it. Men in time dimly guess what time in mists confounds, and God in eternity, with unquenchable and patient hope, awaits the final verdict of the time process. But there is no meeting of God and man, for God is eternal and ineffable whereas man is temporal and phenomenal. It is this which the Bible by implication denies. There is, of course, a metaphysical gulf between God and man, but God can and has bridged the gap, and man in his turn can use the bridge which God has made.

Yet the real gap between God and man is moral and spiritual rather than metaphysical, and it is with this gap that religious proclamation and religious existence are primarily concerned. God, indeed, inhabits eternity, but eternity cannot rightly be defined as mere non-time. Eternity, on the contrary, is a transcendence of time, and the transcendent God, the high and holy one who inhabits eternity, is not excluded by the temporality he transcends, so that the action of God in the midst of the particularities of history and time is neither unthinkable nor impossible. No doubt the divine particularity, God's way of not being anything that he has made, must be distinguished in kind from the particularity which we and events in time possess, yet they are sufficiently akin for the one to be made manifest in the other. Certainly God cannot be imprisoned in mere timeless, spaceless universality. He is not one who can be symbolized but never known, vaguely apprehended everywhere but never met face to face anywhere. To the Bible, God is not merely a remote ground of history but an actual character in history, or rather he is both at the same time, transcendent and immanent, ultimate and proximate, here and now and yet everywhere in general, above us, beneath us, and beside us.

At least we may conclude from all this that there is a close relationship between the philosophy of history and the philosophy of religion. If we are not to take a historical view of religion, then we can hardly take a religious view of history. Only if God can really act in history can man significantly exist before God in eternity.

CHAPTER 4

THE BIBLE AND THE HISTORIANS

WE have already alluded to the distinction—we might almost call it the tension—between being biblical about history (in the sense of history B) and being historical (in the sense of history A) about the Bible. Of course, in one sense either emphasis involves bringing history and the Bible into close relation with each other. But in the first case we take the Bible to be sovereign in relation to historical interpretation, whereas in the second case we take the historical method to be sovereign in relation to biblical interpretation. In the modern world, as we have seen, Arnold Toynbee has been selected as the best and most persuasive example of an effort to be biblical about history, even though we have felt compelled to deplore his reliance upon conventional nineteenth-century comparative religion and philosophy of religion rather than upon biblical theology. The reverse tendency, its use of the historical method as the key or clue to scientific biblical interpretation, is much more common and takes the form of what is usually referred to as 'biblical criticism.'

Biblical criticism implies a critique of the Bible and the biblical sources, both historical and intellectual, rather than a criticism of the Bible in the sense in which the dramatic correspondent of a newspaper may write a criticism of a new play. The aim of the modern biblical critic is to understand a book of the Bible, or even a particular passage in one of the books, in relation to its historical context, to extra-biblical, religious, and intellectual sources, and to the traditions of the Bible itself. It is an effort to understand rather than to appreciate and estimate the value of the Bible, although, of course, such an appreciation or estimation may emerge out of and be consequent upon the scholar's particular interpretation of it.

Nowadays, with the exception of places of learning dominated by fundamentalism—and in their own way such places can be surprisingly learned—this 'critical' way of studying scripture has established itself, almost universally, as the one truly scientific, modern way, and it is now accepted without question in most or our seminaries and theological academies.

For this very reason a philosophical critique of the criticism has become an imperative necessity. Unfortunately almost no one attempts such an ambitious undertaking but the fundamentalists, and their bias in the matter is of such a character as to prevent them from carrying out this urgent task in a way likely to be taken seriously by people outside their own ranks. This is really a vast field of philosophical analysis which calls for a whole book to itself, but in a volume entitled *Towards a Theology of History* the topic can hardly be ignored. In this chapter we can do little more than outline the character of such a philosophical critique. It will not be my purpose here to attempt to refute or crusade against the 'critical' method of studying scripture. Rather I shall try to indicate its basic philosophical affiliations and its consequent limitations and shortcomings. The trouble about biblical criticism is not so much what it succeeds in doing, and for the most part in doing well, as in what it fails to do; not because of any lack of intelligence and ability among the biblical scholars, nor even because of a prevailing paucity of data which renders insight impossible, but rather because of certain characteristic philosophical postulates and affiliations which render it impossible for a man conscientiously adhering to the conventions and methodological rules of self-consciously modern history quite to come to grips with some of the basic biblical themes. In other words, we have to consider not what modern biblical criticism fails to do, so to speak, accidentally, but what it cannot do essentially, because it is the kind of 'blunt' instrument that it is.

Just as modern history studies past events in entire abstraction from any doctrine of providence, so the modern biblical historian scrutinizes and analyses the scriptures in entire abstraction from any doctrine of biblical inspiration. Of course, the historian may himself accept in some sense or other both a doctrine of providence and a doctrine of biblical inspiration, but not in such a manner as to influence in any way his performance as a historian. Perhaps he might argue that a judgement that the history of the world is providentially ordered is something which history A itself might conceivably necessitate and demonstrate by its finished results. The doctrine of providence should come after history, as a kind of meditation upon and evaluation of the results of historical investigation. Similarly the biblical historian might urge that the judgement that the Bible is inspired is one that must be prompted by some picture of the Bible which biblical criticism might conceivably provide. But to say this is to postpone the affirmation of either providence or inspiration to the Greek Kalends or the end of the world, for in the nature of the case the task of the world historian and the biblical historian is chronically inconclusive and can never be brought to an end. In fact, of course, the doctrines of providence and biblical inspiration are affirmed prior to and independently of history and on other than historical grounds, just like the doctrine of progress or the Marxist doctrine of the dialectic of history. Hypotheses of this kind are not demonstrated by historical research—or, for that matter, refuted by historical research—rather they are initial or even *a priori* judgements which assert in one way or another that the field of historical inquiry is one which makes sense and which will well repay a rational analysis. The alternative doctrine, that the field of historical inquiry is a mere procession of endless novelties which have no shape and make no sense whatever, we have already examined.

Before we embark upon the venture of trying to be rational about something or other, we must have the initial conviction that it is the kind of thing that it is possible and worthwhile to be rational about. Providence, progress, and the Marxist dialectic are all of them different, although curiously kindred, ways of insisting upon this very thing. Historical research neither demonstrates nor refutes any of them, although it may very well presuppose any one of these doctrines, or something else of rather the same kind. Usually the something else of rather the same kind takes the form of historical naturalism, a curious and paradoxical, almost self-contradictory notion which we will examine more carefully a little later on.

It is important to add that whatever the presupposition of the historian may be, it should not be one which biases or embarrasses him in the course of his work. Rather it should make possible for him insights and modes of understanding which would otherwise be out of the question. In serious intellectual work of any kind it is impossible to avoid presuppositions. The important distinction in modern thought and research is not the distinction between men with presuppositions and men without presuppositions. There are no men without presuppositions. We carry on from where we are. Some people, like Rene Descartes, the so-called 'father of modern philosophy,' are foolish enough to cherish the idea of erasing the past and starting all over again from the beginning, but this is something we never really succeed in accomplishing. The really important distinction is that between men who do not know what their presuppositions are, and may even try to deny that they have any, and men who are conscious of their presuppositions, who have selected them from various alternative possibilities, who are even willing to defend them when called upon to do so, and find in them not only a basis for their work but a continual source of guidance and insight in their work. Rational beings must learn to presuppose consciously.

Inevitably and properly the presuppositions of any particular science or form of inquiry are not themselves a part of that science or form of inquiry. Thus the presuppositions of physics are not physical, just as the presuppositions of history are not historical. At a first remove the presuppositions of any particular science or form of inquiry would appear to be philosophical, although more ultimately, as was shown conclusively by that great detector and analyst of presuppositions, the late R. G. Collingwood,[1] they turn out to be theological. Of course, it is important to add that atheism and agnosticism are just as much theological presuppositions as theism. Atheism wants to insist that whatever it is that we must ultimately postulate, e.g. the dialectic of history or the order of nature, is in no sense to be identified with the God who is worshipped by religious men. Agnosticism wishes to assert that God, even if he exists, never reveals himself by taking any initiative, never makes any difference to anything else and may therefore safely be ignored for all practical purposes. Theism wants to assert not only that God exists but that he can never be ignored without major error, that, in fact, he makes all the difference to everything, and that the ultimate is not only the ultimate but also the proximate, that the ground of being is also its culmination, that creation is providence, and that God is Lord of history, if only because he is Lord of everything else.

[1] Cf. *An Essay on Metaphysics*. Oxford, 1940. Part IIIA: especially chapters 19 and 20.

Certainly we can never escape from theology merely by saying that God does not exist. This may be only a way of saying something that is theologically true (i.e., that God is not any of the things that merely exist, and that he is not to be equated with anything that is less than himself). Nor can we escape from theology merely by saying that the divine existence makes no difference to anything else, for this is to saddle ourselves with a doctrine of utterly ineffable, ultimate being which can be approached, if at all, only in some kind of wordless, inarticulate mysticism. The Christian will probably say that the atheist is nearer to the truth than the agnostic, but he must insist that both of them have something very important, however in itself inaccurate and misleading, to say about God.

The trouble is that so many of our modern forms of thought and research, in fact, presuppose either atheism or agnosticism, and this is often true even when the thinker or researcher who in other moods, when he is not concerned with the object of his thought or research, is a believing Christian or a religious man of some other kind. So we have the paradox of Christian historians who carry on historical research in total abstraction from any doctrine of providence, and biblical scholars who take no notice in practice of any doctrine of biblical inspiration. The difficulty is that if these doctrines have any truth in them at all they certainly cannot be ignored in any kind of rational practice, and if they have no truth in them whatsoever, we can hardly be justified in professing any kind of Christianity. Of course, we live in a world in which many people are not Christian. There is nothing particularly shocking about that. Christians should be used to it by now. It has always been so in Christian experience, and no doubt will continue to be so. Indeed, with the present and impending huge increase in the world's population the proportion of non-Christians will inevitably increase. The Christians will no doubt increase numerically, but the non-Christians will increase proportionately. In the nature of the case, the missionary responsibilities of the Church can never be fulfilled. To preach the gospel and to teach the faith is a perennial activity. What may concern and scandalize us much more, however, is the spectacle of Christian thinkers and scholars who in the course of their thought and research appear to take no notice of their basic Christian presuppositions.

The doctrine of providence asserts the notion of an ultimate and absolute power which is at the same time magnificently, infinitely tolerant. According to this doctrine, God creates freedom and yet dares to preordain the consummation. To most people this seems something of a paradox, particularly in technological age when men are accustomed to creating instruments for the more or less automatic implementation of their purposes. Except when they beget children it can hardly be said that human beings ever create freedom, although something analogous to the creation of freedom may perhaps be discerned in literature, in really great novels and plays. Most human creations, however, are various types of automata, and the more efficiently we create them the more reliably automatic they are. Yet at a deeper level we may perhaps dimly discern the possibility that to create freedom and yet preordain the consummation may seem less paradoxical to God than it does to us. True, freedom is not the unpredictable irrationality which romantic philosophers have often supposed. On the contrary, true freedom is the power of the rational and the good to endure, to survive, and ultimately to prevail. The clue to the resolution of the paradox is to be seen precisely in the fact that the creation of freedom is essential to the accomplishment of the divine purpose, and that the accomplishment of the divine purpose is equally necessary to the triumph of freedom. Without freedom the Kingdom of God cannot be, and only in the Kingdom of God can freedom attain and maintain its existence with total integrity and security. It is only at first sight that God seems to put his ultimate purpose in jeopardy by creating freedom. Once we begin to comprehend the immensity and magnificence of the purpose we see that the creation of freedom, with all its costly consequences, is absolutely necessary to the total design. This doctrine implies that history will always have direction, point, and shape, because God has preordained the consummation, and yet, on the other hand, that it must inevitably appear haphazard and sporadic, a thing of jerks, fits, and starts, filled with recurrent episodes of tragedy and failure, because the creation of genuine freedom is essential to the attainment of the divine purpose.

In Christian doctrine he who creates also conserves. God hates nothing that he has made, certainly not that element of freedom which is the most glorious characteristic of his creation. Thus the creator of freedom conserves freedom by a steadfast respect for its effectiveness and integrity, by a steadfast respect for human freedom even when it expresses itself in sin and rebellion against the divine purpose, even—and here we come to the heart of Christian devotion—when it nails the incarnate Son of God to the cross. Yet, at the same time, God has indeed preordained the consummation, waiting with massive divine patience for the final hour in which exhausted men will weary of every alternative to the Kingdom of God. Men in their freedom can devise many alternatives to the Kingdom of God. What they cannot do, of course, is make a lasting success of any of them. This observation is the clue which enables us to perceive the possibility that he who creates freedom may nevertheless venture with confidence to preordain the consummation.

Another almost equally important characteristic of the doctrine of providence is the way in which it provides us with the antithesis of any kind of fatalism. The one thing which we cannot suppose with any credibility at all is the notion that man is lord of and uniquely responsible for his own history. Man knows genuine freedom but certainly not absolute or unlimited freedom. He is certainly not in total charge down here. If the visitor from another planet says to us, 'Take me to your leader,' it will not do to take him to some important and powerful human dignitary. It might be better to take him to church. Our real choice is between a doctrine of providence according to which man is controlled by a power infinitely superior to himself which wills and ordains his freedom and his glory, or a doctrine of fate, according to which he is controlled by impersonal forces infinitely inferior to himself which tend inevitably toward his subjection and frustration. Providence or the reign of personality; fate, or the dictatorship of the impersonal; this is our choice. Marxist history, for example, is fateful history, though in a foggy, Victorian way it somehow contrives to attribute to the impersonal dictatorship some at least of the benevolent purposes of God. Christian history, on the other hand, is providential or personal history; it sees history as essentially that which invites, indeed, calls out for, prophecy, and is incomplete without revelation. Most modern history, however, is neither fateful nor providential, but an oscillation between the two, the presuppositions of which are confused; sometimes providence, sometimes fate, and sometimes that confused humanistic idea of man alone over history, in history, and responsible for history which, philosophically speaking, is inferior to both fateful history and providential history alike.

Yet, nevertheless, this last is the kind of history which many biblical scholars think it necessary to emulate, even when they are dealing with the Bible itself. As a result we often have the strange paradox of an interpretation of the Bible for which God himself is not an active factor in the process, in which he takes no initiative, and makes no difference to the general specifications of the course of events. In the Bible itself God is the living God who acts, but many of our recent and contemporary biblical scholars in effect substitute for the Living God who acts the *idea of the Living God who acts,* and are so inept at philosophy and theology as to suppose that the one is identical with the other.[1] But we must insist that the *idea of the Living God who acts* does not act. Ideas never do. The heart of the Bible is not the idea of the Living God who acts but the living God who acts. For the modern historical method it is important that God must never be allowed to do anything. Men may act in relation to or under the influence of their ideas of God, but God himself never passes out of the realm of idea into the realm of concrete action. Thus, for example, God does not inspire the prophets and apostles. Rather the prophets and apostles out of their experience and genius depict and symbolize God. It is unfortunate that they depict and symbolize God as the God who acts, for this really means that, from the point of view of the historical method conventional in the modern world, the prophets and the apostles were really mistaken, and this is, in fact, the true implication, rarely confessed or acknowledged, of course, of modern biblical scholarship.

This is perhaps the first clear example of the general thesis that the conventions of modern historical method make it impossible to come to terms with the basic biblical themes. Here we have a true paradox. Modern biblical scholarship is curiously un-biblical. It is so anxious to be good modern history that it fails to be faithful to biblical history. But the implications of our argument take us further than merely saying that the modern historical

[1] See Appendix to Chapter 4, p. 123.

method is not very good at interpreting the Bible. We have to add that for similar reasons it is really not very good at interpreting anything else. For example, a form of church history which is pursued in total abstraction from the notion of any inspiration of the church in the course of its history is just as defective as the biblical scholarship which abstracts itself entirely from any doctrine of biblical inspiration. Of course, we must agree that this kind of historical scholarship has been chiefly concerned to try and get us beyond mere fundamentalism in biblical studies and mere traditionalism in churchmanship, and in this it has rendered us good service. Mere fundamentalism and mere traditionalism seem to regard the category of inspiration as the only category we require in order to interpret scripture or church history. This is not the case, because men with their finitude and sin are involved in the composition of the Bible and the history of the church just as truly and actively as God is involved. We need both the categories of modern history and of inspiration in order to do justice to the phenomena with which we are confronted. The upshot of this whole movement in contemporary Christendom is that the modern ways of studying and interpreting the Bible and church history, which ought by now to have delivered us completely from both mere fundamentalism and mere traditionalism is provoking so many fundamentalist and traditionalist reactions by the one-sided way in which it brought about the deliverance that it is endangering even the good work that it has accomplished. It is now becoming necessary to revive and restate the doctrine of inspiration. If there really is an element of inspiration running through human history, then history, if it is to be accurate and valid, had better take note of it and make full allowance for it.

But we must go even further. We are not pleading merely that the doctrine of inspiration is an essential category when we are studying the Bible and church history which can be dispensed with everywhere else. Contemporary theologians have made too much use of their distinction between holy or salvation history and secular history. This antithesis is a modern version, no doubt, of St. Augustine's distinction between the City of God and the City of Man. But for St. Augustine himself the City of God is not merely the church, any more than the City of Man is merely the world. In the same way salvation history is no more merely biblical history, or possibly biblical history plus church history, than secular history is merely the history of everything else. At a deeper analysis all secular history is salvation history, for it is the history of what salvation saves. Ultimately both kinds of history call for the employment of the same categories.[1] Perhaps an Aristotelian thinker might say that the City of Man or secular history is the matter of history, whereas the City of God or salvation history is its form. Man is saved in the world, and the world is saved in the salvation of man. The way in which this occurs is the central historical as well as the central theological theme, and we can no more leave the God who acts and saves out of secular history than we can leave him out of salvation history.

This is perhaps the central contention that the author of this book has in mind when he declares that it is more urgent and important to be biblical about history than to be historical about the Bible. The true reconciliation of

[1] The distinction between secular history and salvation history (Geschichte and Heilsgeschichte) is not, of course, to be found in the Bible itself. On the other hand, the data for such a distinction are certainly found in the Bible but in such a way as prevents us from interpreting and defining it as absolute or ultimate. 'Have I not brought up Israel out of the land of Egypt, and the Philistines from Caphtor, and the Syrians from Kir?' (*Amos* 9. 7). A quotation of this kind should be contrasted with: 'You only have I known of all the families of the earth' (*Amos* 3. 2) or 'He hath not dealt so with any nation' (*Psalm* 147. 20). The Bible thus makes a real distinction between the history of the chosen people and that of other nations, but nevertheless insists that God is Lord of both strands of history alike.

the historical and the biblical mind is to be found not so much in a scholarly activity which is historical about the Bible as in a prophetic activity which is biblical about mankind.

Let us now turn to the theory of inspiration. We have already glanced at this theory in one of its most popular and perhaps unacceptable forms, the idea of some kind of verbal dictation of the Bible, and this we have set aside as having more in common with Mohammedan ideas about the Koran than with Christian ideas about the Bible. The very phrase 'verbal inspiration' is a misleading one, for it is obviously not words which are inspired but the people who utter them. What really inspires the speaker is his theme. Inspiration is not intoxication with words but a total surrender to the reality with which the words are concerned. In this sense inspiration, as we find it in the Bible and the history of the church, is at least continuous with, an extension of, the same kind of thing as, inspiration as we find it in the arts. The inspired man is utterly obsessed by, possessed with, dominated and overcome by, used by his theme. His truth has made him free. When a man's theme is God, and when he is utterly surrendered to it, and enslaved by it, then we say that he is inspired, so that it is no longer the man who speaks about his truth out of his genius and experience, but rather God, the Living Truth, who speaks through him. The biblical writers, like the artist in the great hour in which a masterpiece is born, are still themselves, yet at the same time raised above themselves by the power and vitality of their theme. The theme which inspires the Old Testament prophet is the living God of Israel. Similarly the theme which inspires the New Testament writer, intoxicates, possesses and dominates him, is that great act of the living God in the midst of human history which we call Jesus Christ. To be possessed and used by such a theme as this is to be possessed indeed. The words which such men

98

speak in such an hour are, of course, in one sense their own, but in a deeper sense they are the Words of God, the words in which their theme delivers up itself, lays itself bare to human eyes and ears, makes itself manifest where it was not manifest, bringing to light the things hidden in the darkness. For, indeed, this darkness is not the absence of light, but rather the presence of the dazzling light which ordinarily makes men blind. In short, the biblical writers are truly inspired by their theme, and their theme is the living God who gives life and creates freedom.

The biblical interpreter is perhaps closest to the historian of the arts. He must use the ordinary, conventional, historical method, for he has to answer questions like: 'Why in this language?' and 'Why in this particular form, which no doubt it strains and elevates, but from which it nevertheless departs?' The episode occurred in history and therefore it has a historical *milieu*, a context apart from which it cannot be explained. In a sense all historical explanation is explanation *in situ*, interpreting distinct episodes as functions of their background, as unintelligible apart from a knowledge of their background. But the historian of the arts has also to reckon with the factors which give the masterpiece universal relevance and permanence. The masterpiece is not for an age but for all time. Thus there were many composers contemporary with Mozart and Beethoven whose music has been entirely forgotten, yet the mere interpretation of their work *in situ* would be identical with our interpretation of Mozart and Beethoven. The historian of the arts has to allow for an element which is not *in situ*, which is not derived from the surrounding historical *milieu*. This is the element which he calls inspiration. In the same way the biblical interpreter must indeed locate the biblical documents *in situ*. Thus, for example, the context of the Old Testament is the mythological paganism characteristic of the countries bordering on or adjacent to the Mediterranean in the first and second millenniums B.C., but the Old Testament writings are far more than merely functions of their context. We have to allow for another factor that completely transforms all that they borrow from their *milieu* and gives them that kind of permanence and universal relevance that the art historian may find in the symphonies of Beethoven, the plays of Shakespeare or the paintings of Fra Angelico. This is inspiration, the transcendence of context.

The more magnificent the achievement, the more woefully inadequate is the interpretation which is merely *in situ*. The works of man in his mediocrity can be interpreted quite successfully by the merely *in situ* method, but the works of man under inspiration never. The same element can be found in church history. It is quite in vain to interpret the formulation of the creeds and the decisions of the councils of the early Church simply as the result of an effort to think out the meaning of the gospel in terms of Greek metaphysics. In one sense this is just what it was, but in another and even more important sense, it was a process in which the gospel remained triumphantly the gospel, and Greek metaphysics was strained beyond itself, almost beyond recognition, and became an incomparably higher instrument of metaphysical and existential thought and analysis, something which was no longer merely for an age, but of incomparable value for all time. Explanation in terms of inspiration becomes necessary precisely at the point at which explanation *in situ* is clearly seen not to be enough. Inspiration is that element in human history which conventional modern historiographers cannot allow for, the point at which the accepted stock of categories breaks down. To put it briefly in the language characteristic of this book, history B exhausts history A. Real history inevitably transcends any particular historiographical technique of studying and interpreting it. It is thus both the glory and the frustration of the biblical historian that he is dealing with inspired documents, for if he is a modern historian, inspiration is just not one of his categories.

Of course, it is certainly the case that to study the scriptures in abstraction from any doctrine of biblical inspiration, and general history and church history in abstraction from any doctrine of providence, would be a perfectly satisfactory way of proceeding if Christianity and Christian theology had no grasp upon or insight into any part of the truth at all, or if it could be validly supposed that the inspiration of scripture would make no difference to scripture and the activity of providence no difference to actual history. In other words the modern historical treatment of these subjects would be perfectly satisfactory if we were to make the assumption that religion in general and Christianity in particular are altogether false and misleading and have no relationship to any truth whatsoever. This, of course, might conceivably be the case, and in the past arguments have been advanced— and any Christian thinker could easily conceive or imagine even better ones than those that have been actually advanced—in defence of this very radical hypothesis. It is hardly, however, the kind of assumption to which the historian ought to permit himself to be tied down. Indeed, the negative presupposition, the presupposition that whatever may be the case, something or other certainly cannot be the case, is not a true presupposition at all. At best it is a dogma, at worst it is a prejudice. Of course, negative dogmas of this kind may be valid, and prejudices may sometimes be justified, but only in comparatively rare and exceptional cases, of which historical research is certainly not one.

Inevitably no Christian theologian would hold that Christian theology or any other kind of human intellectualism grasps the whole truth exactly and entirely, but he would hold that all the great historic preoccupations of the human intellect have in one way or another some grasp upon and relationship to truth, each in its own appropriate way, and that theology in its own analogical manner apprehends something of the truth about God and the modes of the divine activity in creation and providence which is much too important to be overlooked or ignored. Again, very formidable arguments have been advanced in the past on behalf of this hypothesis, and no doubt even more compelling and persuasive arguments will be put forward in the future. That this hypothesis has its measure of validity and truth would be a genuine and tenable presupposition. That it has no measure of truth at all is a bogus presupposition, which most absolutely ought not to be presupposed. What is quite unthinkable is the idea that the doctrines of inspiration and providence, even if true, would make no difference to history and historical method, so that they can be safely ignored by the historian. Of course, the labours of the historian cannot demonstrate or validate that either of these doctrines is true. The most the historian could do would be to verify them somewhat by showing that better and more insightful history can be thought and written on the basis of such presuppositions than can be thought and written without them. This would slightly increase the favourable evidence at our disposal, but it would not itself demonstrate or conclusively prove the validity of the presuppositions. In fact, we never prove or demonstrate our presuppositions. We merely in certain cases discover and verify their usefulness in practice.

We conclude from this discussion that the modern historical approach is only valid if Christianity and Christian doctrine, or something rather like them, is totally untrue. If they have any truth in them at all, then there is something very wrong indeed with the intellectual make-up and 'mental set' of contemporary historical man.

From this point we may perhaps consider what have been in fact the philosophical affiliations and presuppositions of modern historiography. The historical movement of thought in the modern world begins in Germany at the end of the eighteenth century and made its heavy impact upon modern culture through the work of the great German historians and biblical scholars during the nineteenth century. It thus coincided almost exactly in time with the flourishing of the great modern German philosophers, who have done so much to influence and modify the whole climate of intellectual opinion right down to our own day. Behind the German historians and biblical scholars, and, because of their tremendous influence, all modern historians and biblical scholars, loom the shadows of Kant and Hegel, and their successors all the way down to Husserl and Heidegger. We can show this very clearly by analysing very briefly two contemporary trends in biblical scholarship. I refer here to 'Form Criticism' allied to the Kerygma theology—which I will call biblical Kantianism—and the 'myth' theology—which I will call biblical Hegelianism. These are, indeed, not the only examples which might be cited, but for our purposes they seem very much the best.

Kerygma theology begins with what looks like a perfectly valid and feasible historical question. What was the form and content of the gospel armed with which the earliest Christian church first confronted the world and embarked upon its history-changing propagandas? After all, this was the kind of question with which the reformers began their work in the sixteenth century. If it is the case, and in so far as it is the case, that the teachings of the contemporary catholic church diverge in any way from the original Kerygma of the earliest church, then, they assumed, we are confronted with a scandalous situation which warrants the most emphatic protests and can even justify schism. Luther, for example, supposed

that he had discovered the form and content of the earliest
Kerygma in the invention of his phrase 'justification by
faith.' On that he stood because he could do no other.
The modern Lutheran biblical scholar may or may not
be convinced that Luther was quite right in all this, but
at least he asks a similar question and seeks a similar
solution. We can see this discussion being carried on in
ecclesiastical controversy throughout the seventeenth and
eighteenth centuries, but it is only in the nineteenth and
twentieth centuries that it becomes philosophically important. Once we have answered the question about the
form and content of the original Kerygma to our own
satisfaction then we can begin to interpret this as a valid
insight into the mind of the earliest church, and to consider the way in which the interests, needs and necessities
of the first-century church influenced and dictated the
actual form and content of the New Testament documents.

It is here that the Kantian presuppositions of all this
begin to appear. What the New Testament documents
inform us about, and what the biblical scholars grasp and
interpret, is not the figure of the Christ himself, but the
attitudes towards Christ and the beliefs about Christ
widely current and taken for granted in the earliest
church. According to the doctrines expounded in the
Kantian critiques, men never know the thing, the object
of experience, as it is in itself. The noumenon or 'thing in
itself' is forever unknown to us. All we can know is the
thing as it is apprehended by minds equipped by the
characteristic categories and limitations which dominate
human experience. The experience is not the experience
of the object, rather it is the experience of the impact of
the object upon the experiencing mind. This dualism
between the thing as it really is, upon the one hand, and
the experience of the thing upon the other, with the
implication that the relationship between the two is a
mystery which cannot even be guessed at, is a general

characteristic of eighteenth-century philosophers, even those whose views differ widely from Kant's. For example, in Locke and Hume as well as in Kant, greatly though they differ from him in so many ways, experience again and again turns out not to be experience of anything so much as experience of experience, which may or may not have any relationship to real things. The world was thus bifurcated into real things on the one hand and our ideas about them on the other, and nobody could possibly succeed in conclusively demonstrating that there was any necessary relationship between the two.

Thus, from the point of view of this kind of biblical scholarship, what we know and is communicated in the New Testament is not the actual figure of Jesus but the mind of the early Church. The actual figure of Jesus has got to be conjectured out of what we know of the mind of the early Church, just as, for example, according to a British empiricist like Hume, the actual face of the world about us has got to be conjectured and projected out of a somewhat confused and incoherent mass of sense data. Men do not really experience the world, they themselves construct and project their own picture of the world. All they have to go upon are the sense data, which are the fragments or atoms of their own experience. No doubt Kant did a much better job on this than Locke or Hume or any British empiricist, but basically he still adhered to the same patterns and presuppositions. We never experience the real world. We only experience our own experience of the real world. And that owes at least as much, if not more, to the way in which our minds are constituted as to the actual characteristics of the real world.

Thus I describe as biblical Kantianism this doctrine that what we know in the New Testament is not Jesus himself, but the mind of the earliest Church. Of course, the question which Kant never formulated or confronted is precisely the question whether there is anything to be said about the structure and ways of reason as man knows them which enables us to assert that the mind of man is in some way adequate to the content of his experience, so that of human experience at least we can say that it is not merely experience of human experience, but experience *of* a real world. Hegel did envision this question and he attempted to provide a strongly positive answer, even though it was not perhaps an entirely satisfactory one. But Kant never even got around to asking the question.

So far as the New Testament is concerned, our answer has already been implied by our brief sketch of the doctrine of inspiration. In an important sense the mind of the earliest church really was the mind of Christ. He so dominated and informed it that it was adequate for the purpose of descrying and interpreting him as he was in history and truly is in eternity. Of course, this process in and through which Christ dominated the mind of the early Church was a lengthy one and it produced much more than the New Testament documents. We find it continuing in later centuries in the decisions of the councils and the composition of the creeds. We can no more afford to set up any artificial barrier between the New Testament and the formulation of doctrine in the catholic church than we dare set up a similar barrier between Jesus himself and the New Testament documents. Just as sight sees what it sees and not the process of vision—actually sight never sees the process of vision—so the New Testament documents present Jesus, and not the mind of the early Church. Actually it is the mind of early Church rather than the so-called 'Jesus of History' which has to be constructed and projected by the New Testament scholar. The odd thing is that we still labour with a kind of biblical and historical Kantinaism long after philosophy has ceased to be dominated by Kant himself, so that Kant survives in the presuppositions of historical methodology more surely and effectively than in his own three great critiques.

Certainly even modern philosophy finds it difficult altogether to release itself from the dualistic consequences and attitudes of the post-Cartesian eighteenth-century philosophy—for example, it is still influential in a good deal of linguistic analysis—but in general most of us have contrived to return to a healthy realism about experience which willy-nilly we have to tolerate in real life and cannot therefore altogether ignore in real philosophy.

Hegel's way of getting out of the difficulty was to declare that, after all, the chief characteristic of the human experiencing mind is reason. But reason is not only characteristic of the human experiencing mind, it is also the chief characteristic of what is there to be experienced. 'Reason is the very substance of reality.' Hence the potentialities of human experiencing are parallel and adequate to the realities that have to be experienced. A not unsimilar doctrine was advanced as early as Plato. All experience is experience *of* rational reality *by* rational beings. Hence our experience is experience of the thing in itself after all. This was a great insight and it was perhaps the only way in which German philosophy could move significantly beyond Kant.

Unfortunately the actual movements beyond Kant which Hegel proceeded to make were much more open to question than his original insight. What do we mean when we say that the reality that we experience is as basically rational as the mind that does the experiencing? For Hegel this meant a new variation on the old doctrine that the structure of logic, the laws of thought, are the same as the laws of reality. Hegel's logic is dialectical. Dialectic is a word used by Plato, but Hegel gave it a new twist. According to him dialectical thinking is a movement from thesis through antithesis to synthesis. We should all agree that this is a way in which thought sometimes operates, but Hegel believed that this is the way in which it always and inevitably operates, at least whenever it operates efficiently. From this it is but a short step to the view that not only does thought move dialectically, but reality moves dialectically also, for the laws of thought are the laws of being. The influence of this doctrine, not only upon history and biblical scholarship, but also upon Marxism, is well known. To historicize efficiently is to discover again and again dialectical processes in actual courses of events, for example, the inevitable movement from class conflict to a classless society. In most cases these Hegelian motifs now belong to the past history of modern thought. Contemporary thinkers, apart from the Marxists, no longer indulge in them. Communism is still very much with us as a historical movement, but Marxist thought is a kind of musty Victorianism, to which respect is no longer paid except in Marxist countries, and then only in a ritual kind of way.

However, one relic of Hegelianism at least still survives in modern biblical scholarship. If the doctrine that all the assertions recorded in the New Testament are literally true represents thesis, the radical notion that they are all literally untrue represents antithesis. We can then move on triumphantly to the grand synthesis according to which the records and assertions of the New Testament are mythically true. This does not necessarily imply that they are literally and historically untrue, but it is nevertheless quite compatible with such an assertion. This particular application of Hegelian ideas was first introduced into New Testament scholarship by David Strauss in his book *Leben Jesu* (first published in two volumes in 1835 and 1836), but it has survived and by many contemporaries it is supposed to represent almost the latest development in New Testament theology. Thus we may call it, not unjustly, biblical Hegelianism. The odd thing is that its

most famous contemporary representative Rudolf Bultmann is not in philosophy a Hegelian at all, but a follower
of Martin Heidegger. It is all rather mixed up and none
the better for that. Bultmann's foundations are Hegelian
though his superstructure is architectured on quite a
different basis.

The question for us is not so much whether this is a
good and useful way of using and applying Hegelian concepts. It is certainly no worse than any other. The real
question is whether, at this time of day, we want to use
and apply any Hegelian concepts at all, particularly in a
structure of thought which delights to think of itself as,
above all, contemporary. Is it really true that the doctrine
that reality is rational implies that the laws of reality are
the laws of thought? that the structure of reality is
dialectical? Surely the adequacy of reason, the capacity
of reason to grasp and interpret experience, could be
supported in quite another way. After all, it was still true
that, even for Hegel, thought could only think itself,
reason could only grasp the rational, and in this sense
Hegel was still, like Kant, a prisoner of the eighteenth
century. We can at least concede the alternative view
that the grandeur of reason is to be found precisely in its
power to grasp and even to make sense of the non-
rational, perhaps even the irrational, if we suppose that
anything that deserves to be described as the downright
irrational actually exists, which is perhaps a meaningless
supposition. Now the intrinsically non-rational certainly
exists, but we only know that it exists by reasoning. It
would appear that reason can grasp the non-rational after
all, that it is capable of making sense of other things
besides itself. How else could we have a rational psychia-
try and abnormal psychology? through which even the
ravings of a lunatic can be rationally interpreted, not
interpreted, of course, in such a way to suggest that really
or deep down they are rational after all, but rather in a

way that makes sense of even their stark irrationality. Even if we allow to Hegel's insight more validity than this, it by no means follows that all rational processes, whether in the mind or in the real course of events, are dialectical in the Hegelian sense. In fact, there may be genuinely rational processes which are non-dialectical, at least in elementary mathematics, and conversely there may be many applications of Hegel's dialectical method which are not really rational, for example, the mythic idea which we have borrowed from David Strauss and which plays so large a part in contemporary mythic theology. The main point of this discussion is that the mythic kind of theology which we find in Bultmann has no real attractions except for a basically Hegelian mind. We happen to live in an age in which there are no basically Hegelian minds to speak of, nor have we any reason to suppose that this particular intellectual species is likely to experience any kind of resurrection from the dead. Even Bultmann is not really Hegel *redivivus*. He is merely Hegel perversely surviving long after his time, and in a cruelly perverse and unresponsive context.

But perhaps by far the most important philosophical influence on biblical scholarship and interpretation has been the kind of philosophy known as naturalism. Naturalism is certainly not Hegelian in the sense that Hegel himself would have approved of it or taught anything remotely like it. On the other hand, it is certainly a monistic doctrine, related to Hegel's absolute idealism in very much the same way as Marxist dialectical materialism is related to absolute idealism. Naturalism, like dialectical materialism, is a kind of inverted, deflated Hegelianism. Indeed, dialectical materialism is really one form of naturalism, and it is characteristic of Hegelianism that it was able to produce these left-wing parodies of itself. Hegel would have not approved of this particular baby, but he could hardly disclaim paternity.

The vogue of naturalism in the modern world, particularly among the less gifted and profound of our philosophers, is a kind of by-product of the tremendous and, indeed, justly earned prestige of the sciences. In an age when the mass of men think much more highly of the natural sciences than of other modes of study and research, the professors and devotees of what we may call the non-scientific studies may be tempted to try to dress up their researches and inquiries in a verbal costume that makes them look as much like science as possible. This is why we are plagued with systems of naturalistic history, positivistic philosophy and mechanistic sociology. The results of such undertakings are perhaps hardly science in the most generally accepted sense of the word, but at least they conspire to suggest that the authors, if not scientists, are at least fellow-travellers with science.

Professor Sorokin, in his famous and useful textbook *Contemporary Sociological Theories*,[1] parodies all such tendencies amusingly in his mythical conception of a 'physics of the ten-cent cigar.'[2] Obviously, if the ten-cent cigar is a phenomenon which can be completely and exhaustively interpreted by the laws of physics, then we do not need any special 'physics of the ten-cent cigar.' If, on the other hand, we do need a special 'physics of the ten-cent cigar' that necessity clearly implies that the categories of physical science are unable to do justice to the actuality of the ten-cent cigar. Obviously the ten-cent cigar is a popular commodity which demands to be explained not only in terms of physics but also in terms of the customs of a particular culture in which tobacco-smoking is a widespread habit, and also in terms of the economics of a particular society with a particular form of currency and a particular price level. Years later, for example, inflation or a rise in the prices of raw materials, possibly due to a

---

[1] Harper and Bros., 1928.   [2] Op. cit., p. 30 f.

rise in the wages of tobacco-workers, will have transformed the ten-cent cigar into a twenty-five-cent cigar without any improvement in its quality.

There is, of course, no special physics of the ten-cent cigar. The very idea is not only a parody but a parable. The great error of mechanists and naturalists and people of that kind is that of literalizing their analogies and their images, very much as the fundamentalists do in the realm of biblical interpretation. There may, indeed, be times when it is useful to think of physical nature in terms of the analogy with the machine, or to describe the history of a particular society by means of a similar analogy with the organism. But, obviously, the physical world is not a machine, and just as obviously a patch of history, however complete in itself, is not an organism. This means, of course, that nature is not mechanical and that history is not organic. There is no harm in using the analogies provided we are not deceived by the success with which we do so into supposing that they are literal truths. Similarly there is no harm in saying that we must look up to behold the majesty of God, so long as we are careful to remember that the phrase is a purely analogical one which in no way implies that God is really up there in space. That we must never literalize our images, or mistake our analogies for factual reports, has long been regarded as one of the first and basic rules of theological thought. But it is also an essential rule of historical and sociological thought, especially in an age intellectually bemused by the astonishing success of the scientific method.

Naturalistic historicism proceeds by assuming that the whole field of historical events composes a real kind or class of events, all akin to each other and sharing a single common nature in terms of which they are defined. It is in a way a late child of the ancient Aristotelian logic of classes. According to such a doctrine all genuine historical events must partake of and exemplify this common nature, so that no one of them can be entirely out of line with the others. It can thus easily be used as a kind of *a priori* ground or presupposition on the basis of which we can reject all narratives embodying the miraculous or supernatural whatsoever. Whatever happened, the miraculous or supernatural cannot have happened.

But this notion of a real kind or definable class of historical events calls for more careful analysis. Clearly it is a class which incorporates within its unity an extraordinary area of diversity. For example, stone-age society or an Italian city of the Renaissance, grinding maize into flour by hand and the Eiffel Tower or the nuclear bomb, polyandry and monogamy, the tribal medicine man and the contemporary surgeon, and an innumerable number of contrasts equally great. Indeed, if we are going to take the notion of a real kind or definable class called historical events seriously, then it is more like a genus than a species, more like the class of vertebrates, for example, which includes both Socrates and white leghorns, than like the class of crocodiles. But if the class of historical events is a genus which includes innumerable different species, there is, after all, no particular reason why we should not stretch it to include the species of miraculous or supernatural events. After all, it is difficult to see that virgin birth or virginal conception, for example, differs from ordinary bi-sexual reproduction more sharply than a hydrogen bomb differs from a boomerang. If a real kind or class of historical events is not stretched beyond its limits by the latter contrast, there is no particular reason *a priori* why it should strain so compulsively at the former.

But perhaps it is insufficient when criticizing a philosophical doctrine like naturalism merely to point out that history is obviously not a department of nature, just as

nature itself is obviously not a machine. More fundamentally we must point to the general truth that our
concepts lose their usefulness in their own proper sphere
if we strain and extend them to include too much.
Obviously man is to some extent sovereign in relation to
his concepts, and if we like to say that the realm of nature
includes history, society and culture and the world of
religious behaviour, then, provided we greatly increase
the number of special distinctions to be observed in the
world of nature as thus conceived, no great harm is done,
except to the lucidity and clarity of the concept of nature
itself. Once the word nature has been stretched to include
everything in general it indicates nothing in particular.
Nature is a concept that has very little meaning except
that which it acquires from its proper contrast with the
non-natural or supernatural. Once we make the word
nature a synonym for everything it has no value and
usefulness whatever, except to provide a foundation for a
precarious structure of monistic metaphysics.

In the past 'nature' had a more specific meaning. For
example, in Greek thought it indicated what we may call
the realm of the natures, a world in which we find varied
collections of particular things, each participaitng in or
representing a common form or universal nature in terms
of which any particular collection could be grasped as a
unity and defined. It made very little difference whether
this doctrine of a realm of natures took a Platonic or an
Aristotelian form. In later Christian thought, which
differed sharply from Greek thought despite its great
indebtedness to it, the term nature was more or less identical with the idea of the creation, the realm of contingent
being and secondary causality. It was out of this doctrine
that there emerged the basic assumptions of the modern
scientific method. Since nature is the creation, which
only exists because God so willed, and which, had he
willed otherwise, might either not have existed at all or

existed in a very different form, we can only find out what it is that God has actually chosen to create by using the empirical method. On the other hand, since God is absolute reason as well as absolute will, we can be quite sure from the outset that whatever it is that God has chosen to create will be susceptible of rational interpretation.

It is this combination of empirical and rational methods which has provided modern science with its basic methodological form. Science is neither merely empirical, on the one hand, nor merely rationalistic on the other. The necessity of such a combination was implicit from the first in the biblical doctrine of creation, so that we may say that the special form taken by science in the modern age is the characteristically biblical and Christian form. From this point of view the word nature connotes the proper subject-matter of the natural sciences and it denotes the creation. Nature is simply our name for the creation when considered in itself in abstraction from the correlative notion of the creator. Thus interpreted, the concept of nature, far from providing any foundation for a system of monistic metaphysics, implies, because it is an abstraction which presupposes the correlative idea of the creator, that monistic metaphysics is impossible.

Obviously a historical technique which presupposes any kind of historical naturalism such as we have briefly described cannot do justice to or take seriously many of the most dramatic and significant New Testament assertions. If we treat such assertions as assertions about Jesus they cannot be true. If we treat them as judgements which indicate the mind of the early church, then we can only say that the mind of the early Church must have been profoundly mistaken in its view of Jesus. In a strange way the inverted Hegelianism which we find in naturalism reinforces the more straightforward Hegelianism which we detected in the so-called mythic theology.

It is because narratives involving the miraculous and the supernatural cannot, according to naturalism, possibly be true, that the biblical scholar who wishes to maintain some kind of contact and continuity with the Christian religion is compelled to regard them not as simply untrue but as mythic. We can see this clearly in writers of the Bultmannian school, who are naturalistic enough to reject the miraculous and the supernatural, but yet insist that such narratives are, or at least may be, true and relevant in an existential sense.

What we have tried to show in this chapter is the tremendous influence upon modern historical method of philosophical presuppositions and prejudices which are open to the greatest question, and, upon analysis, vulnerable to profound philosophical criticisms. More particularly, they are so entirely out of line with the whole biblical outlook as to make it quite impossible for such methods to arrive at any genuine biblical interpretation or understanding. From within the biblical tradition we must insist and confidently expect that the more profoundly and validly we understand and interpret the Bible, the greater the religious depth with which it will challenge and speak to us. It is precisely here that modern biblical scholarship has proved itself so insipid and unstimulating. We are confronted with the paradox of a way of studying the word of God out of which no word of God ever seems to come, with an imposing modern knowledge of the Bible which seems quite incapable of saying anything biblical or thinking biblically. Kant and Hegel and other German philosophers always seem to be standing in the background, but the immanent spirit of the Bible itself has long since departed from the scene.

What is required in order to remedy this situation is not a return to fundamentalism, although that seems what we are most likely to get. Our point is not that the Bible is a great surd which requires special historical methods and techniques all to itself, while the existing historical method is perfectly adequate to comprehend everything else in human history. The Bible, after all, is another way of understanding and interpreting not merely biblical history but all history. We should not be comforted greatly by the emergence of a biblical way of understanding the Bible side by side with a non-biblical way of understanding everything else.

Christian thought and theology is confronted by two urgent and major tasks. First of all, to echo a phrase of St. Anselm, the faith must learn to understand itself. Theology, in other words, is concerned, like all other forms of human thought in their own way, with the passage from credibility to intelligibility. Men begin by merely believing and then slowly evolve an understanding of that in which they once merely believed. Thus from the beginning of human time men have believed in the rainbow, but they only began to understand the rainbow at a comparatively recent date. They believed in the existence of babies long before they understood how babies are generated and produced.

For the faith to understand itself, to progress in this way from credibility to intelligibility, is no doubt difficult enough. The job has never been done completely and in all probability never will be done with total success, even though we were allowed infinite time in which to do it. But theology also confronts a second and even more challenging task. It must not only understand itself, it must also seek a parallel understanding of everything else in terms of itself. Thus it is not enough merely to stop being historical, as the modern world understands the historical mind and methodology, about the Bible, and to start being biblical about the Bible. What we have to do is to start being biblical about all history, as the Hebrew prophets were in the ancient world, and as Arnold Toynbee above all others, albeit haltingly and with little understanding of what he was doing, has begun to do in the contemporary world. In other words, the brief critique of historical methodology contained in this chapter applies not only to our somewhat sterile modern biblical scholarship, but also, and perhaps more universally and significantly, to all forms of historical scholarship whatsoever. In terms of philosophical party labels our contention is that historical scholarship is more searching and adequate to the real problems of human history when it is Platonic and biblical in its presuppositions, as in the case of Toynbee, than when, as in the case of most other modern historians, it is Kantian and Hegelian.

There is perhaps one other conception of history associated particularly with contemporary biblical scholarship which calls for mention here before this brief survey is concluded. We refer to the more or less existentialist conception of history closely associated with the Bultmannian movement in biblical scholarship and interpretation which has found expression in Friedrich Gogarten, a philosophical colleague of Bultmann's. According to Gogarten, 'Wherever we have to do with history, we have to do with the historic character of human existence.'[1] By this 'historic character of human existence' he means that man know himself to be responsible for the form of the world. 'I see the constitutive element of history (Geschichte) and that which makes human existence in the world historic in the responsibility of man for the world.'[2] History and the historic must, according to him, be distinguished from the mere facts, which he describes as the 'historical' (*das Historische*). The historic is that in history which challenges us and stimulates us to realize the existential possibilities latent in the historic character (*geschichtlich*) of our existence at the present time. The

[1] Freidrich Gogarten, *Entmythologisierung und Kirche*. 2nd edition, Stuttgart, 1954, p. 45.   [2] Op. cit., p. 10.

historical, on the other hand, merely satisfies an un-existential curiosity about past human events.

It is quite obvious that some past events do have this historic quality which Gogarten ascribes to them, whereas others do not. For example, episodes like the Great Rebellion in the reign of Charles the First, the French Revolution and the American Civil War still to this day divides people in England, France and America and compel them to take sides against one another even when they are engaged in narrating the course of events as accurately and honestly as they can. The historian as he writes will know himself to be a Cavalier or a Roundhead, a Jacobin or a Girondin, a Federal or a Confederate, in the very process of historicizing. Of course, the New Testament story is perhaps, at all events for us in the west, the most outstanding example of the historic in Gogarten's sense. The New Testament story does not compel us to be Christians but it does compel us to be either Christians or non-Christians. By sheer force of its own latent powers it insists that we take one side or the other. Other historical episodes, for example the Wars of the Roses, may have either none of this existential urgency at all or possess it only in a very low and inferior degree.

On the other hand, existential moods and climates of opinion may change profoundly from generation to generation. What was once merely historical may re-emerge as profoundly historic. Thus for most of the nineteenth century the eschatological passages in the New Testament, in which Jesus speaks of a violent end of the world, were merely historical. The historian could say either that Jesus was after all and understandably merely a man of his time, or that these passages, although foreign to his essential message, were intruded into the gospels later because the evangelists who wrote them were merely men of their time. It is only now, when we have to take seriously into account the possibility that the world may after all end not with a whimper but a bang, and that possibly the biblical imagery may be much nearer the literal truth than the liberal minds of our forefathers were capable of supposing, that the eschatological element in the gospels has come alive for us again and now forms, in Gogarten's sense, an essential part of that in the gospels which is historic for us rather than merely historical.

But the real objection to Gogarten's doctrine is not so much that the way in which we draw the lines of distinction between the historic and the historical is so shiftingly subjective, and so to speak occasional. The basic difficulty lies elsewhere. Even though the lines of distinction between the historic and the historical were permanent and indelible, both the historic and the historical would still be embedded in the same course of events. Even the historic is in an important sense historical, and the historical is always at least potentially historic. The historian must insist that both the historic and the historical after all really happened in history, and that he has a right to be equally interested in both. On the other hand, the theologian and the Christian philosopher cannot refrain from pointing out with some emphasis that both the historic and the historical are equally under the providence of God. The distinction between the historic and the historical is no doubt a useful one for some purposes, like the distinction between salvation history and secular history, but it must not be allowed to harden into an absolute dualism. We cannot suppose, for example, that the historic is a course of events immediately related to divine providence whereas the historical has no relationship to divine providence at all. This would be St. Augustine's distinction between the City of God and the City of Man in an even worse form than the modern distinction between salvation history and secular history.

But perhaps the gravest and most astounding error of all in Gogarten's thesis is his notion that the historic character of human existence is its capacity to produce in man a sense of our human responsibility for the form of the world. One would have thought that to sense the nature of historic existence is almost precisely the opposite of this. To know what we are in human history is above all to sense our limitations, to realize that we are *not* responsible for the form of the world. Something intractable in the structure of historic existence is continually frustrating and over-ruling us. It may be something impersonal and inferior to us, in which case we shall conclude for some kind of gloomy fatalism or determinism; on the other hand, it may be something personal or super-personal and infinitely superior to us, in which case we shall conclude for a doctrine of divine providence. One thing, however, is overwhelmingly clear. Men are no more the masters of history than they are the lords of creation. This all-pervading finitude is perhaps the primary and most indelible characteristic of historic existence. In history man meets his match and his master. It is only otherwise in fantasies and dreams.

Biblical scholarship and interpretation in the great classical periods of classical Christian thought was characteristically close to theological thought and the interests of the Christian philosopher, on the one hand, and to the devotional life and the hazards and problems of Christian existence on the other. But modern biblical interpretation, despite the vast erudition and noble intellectual intentions of the scholars themselves, is greatly its inferior in both these dimensions. Theologically and philosophically it is sterile; from the spiritual and existential point of view, it is uninspiring and lacking in spiritual drive or stimulus. In this chapter we have tried to outline and illustrate the reasons for this lamentable failure. So much modern history and biblical interpretation is not only good history, it is also bad philosophy. The weak philosophical presuppositions have blinded the biblical scholars to the glory of the Bible, just as surely as it has concealed the meaning of history from the eyes of the historians. More generally we may say that a chronic incapacity to achieve philosophical understanding on any profound level has been the great weakness of 'modern' thought (using the word 'modern' not in the sense of contemporary or near contemporary but in the more correct sense of 'since the Renaissance'). Scientifically and in so many other ways this modern mind has been so splendidly gifted and so magnificently successful; but its strange weakness in philosophy, a field in which the Greek and medieval worlds were so strong, has prevented it from interpreting correctly its own results and from achieving any critical awareness of its presuppositions. Perhaps it has been the highly exciting quality of science, and more recently of history, which has diverted the mental attention of so many of the ablest minds away from philosophy, and from the great work of seeking any unified interpretation of our total knowledge of the world. We have lost wisdom in the pursuit of science and mislaid understanding in the quest for knowledge. Compared with our Greek and medieval forefathers we know so much more and understand so much less. 'It is the empirical fact,' says Whitehead, 'that process entails loss.'[1] In quantitative terms obviously we modern men have gained infinitely more than we have lost. Qualitatively, however, it may yet be true that we have lost more than we have gained.

[1] *Process and Reality.* Cambridge, 1929, p. 482.

APPENDIX TO CHAPTER 4

Faith in the Living God

OBVIOUSLY any belief in a living God who acts in human history must be combined with and supported by an ability and willingness to point to certain events in history which unmistakably attest to, as well as merely symbolize the divine activity. In the Bible we are sometimes confronted with events in which the Lord God, as the Bible says, 'lays bare his holy arm' and acts, so to speak, nakedly and unmistakably. Here we encounter testimonies to events of a supernatural or miraculous kind, which, if we grant that they have occurred at all, cannot possibly bear any other explanation. Elsewhere we are confronted with a veiled form of divine activity, God acting by working in the hearts of men, inspiring the prophets and the saints, or even moving the minds of men who are anything but prophets or saints to act in a way that conforms with the divine plan. In this latter case it would always be possible, even for those who grant that the events occurred, to reject or ignore the hypothesis of divine activity.

We may say that the naked acts of God manifest the divine transcendence and that the veiled acts of God manifest the divine immanence. However, many theologians and biblical scholars of the so-called 'liberal' type accept only the veiled acts of God and reject what we have called the naked acts. But in that case we must honestly ask ourselves whether we have any basis for what has now become the somewhat superfluous hypothesis of the divine activity. It is always possible for the historian to declare that 'he has no need of that hypothesis,' and to treat the veiled acts of God as though they were merely human acts, often, no doubt, of somewhat extraordinary and exceptional character. In other words, the most important ground of the assertion that God is the 'living God who acts' is to be found not in his veiled activity but in his naked activity. Without the assertion of the naked activity of God the concept of the living God who acts becomes merely an idea, perhaps even a superfluous one which can be eliminated with a stroke of Occam's razor, which some of us employ in order to interpret certain events which could conceivably be interpreted in another, but less uniform, way.

The accustomed category of the historian is not divine action, as in the Bible, but human action. Thus many historians interpret the veiled acts of God as human acts, and deny that the naked acts ever took place at all. Nowhere is the breach between the mind of the Bible and mind of the conventional modern historian more absolutely clear. Nevertheless, unless we point in the biblical way to the naked acts of God, the case for believing in any real divine activity in what we have called the veiled acts becomes very much weakened. For the biblical mind the living God is, above all, revealed in the naked acts. Thus the Resurrection, for example, is declared to be a notorious fact which 'was not done in a corner' (*Acts* 26. 26).

The general tendency of the modern biblical scholars, inspired by peculiar Lutheran doctrines about the nature of the faith, has been to declare that the veiled acts of God are known to be acts of God only by faith. In the Bible it is the naked acts of God that arouse faith, but in a great deal of modern theology it is faith that recognizes that the acts of God are indeed the acts of God. Faith is required because now the only acts of God in question are veiled acts, which could easily, without and apart from faith, be interpreted as human acts. Thus the theologian who is overmuch influenced by the assumptions and prejudices of the modern historical mind may find himself as far removed from the spirit of the Bible as the historian himself.

It must be insisted that faith is neither an organ of apprehension nor a form of thought. Whatever faith recognizes and entrusts itself to originally made itself known to faith in some other way. In Christianity, for example, that which faith confesses made itself known to the man of faith through scripture and through the tradition of the church which testifies to scripture and perpetuates its intrinsic message, and, of course, through theological reasoning about scripture and the traditions of the church. Nothing is known to 'faith alone.'

Indeed, the very idea of 'faith alone' involves a basic misunderstanding of the nature of faith. For faith is an evaluation of knowledge rather than a form or source of knowledge. To some of that which he knows the whole man entrusts and commits himself entirely. It is this total self-commitment which we call faith, this conviction that there are some items of knowledge that are not mere items of knowledge but saving, redeeming facts. Faith embraces these realities and commits itself to them entirely, but that does not mean that they are known to 'faith alone.' Faith does not know anything, rather it commits the whole man to a reality which is known in some other way.

In its extreme forms this belief that 'faith alone' knows the Christian realities and accepts the gospel turns into what is known as *fideism* (which we may define as faith in faith). Thus Gogarten even seems to suppose that the purity of faith would be corrupted if there were any reason outside faith for asserting what faith asserts. 'It would imply a desire to rely upon the world and the context of events within it, if we sought within that context for grounds for the trustworthiness of the tradition' (*Entmythologisierung und Kirche*, p. 77). But this is to demonstrate the irrelevance of faith rather than to preserve its purity. Indeed, faith must have its reasons for asserting what it asserts if it is to be an act of the whole man in his integrity. There is clearly a circularity of reasoning in appealing to faith in order to substantiate the biblical testimonies which are the ground of faith. Faith cannot substantiate our testimonies to the acts of the living God, for it is the acts of the living God that evoke faith. The proper biblical order is: first, the act of the living God which evokes faith; and then the faith which testifies to the act. We can never put it the other way around without being guilty of arguing most ineffectively in a circle.

CHAPTER 5

THE EPISTEMOLOGY OF HISTORY

THERE are two ways of coming to grips with the problems of epistemology, the theory of the form, nature and perhaps the limitations of knowledge. First is the rather *a priori* and abstract way preferred by most modern philosophers, by eighteenth-century English empiricists, by Kantians (perhaps above all by Kantians), and by the positivists. This method attempts rather artificially to examine the structure and possibilities of knowledge before we really begin to know, the idea being that a correct theory of knowledge will enable us to distinguish in advance between what we can know and what we cannot know, between questions which can be answered and questions which cannot be answered, so that we can save ourselves the trouble of prosecuting useless inquiries and bothering ourselves with the contemplation of unanswerable questions. A great deal of contemporary philosophy is not based, like ancient and medieval philosophy, on wonder and unquenchable curiosity, but rather on the refusal to wonder and on a doctrinaire quenching of curiosity. The second method, characteristic of ancient and medieval philosophers, begins by taking note of what it is that we do in fact know, and then inquiring how it is that we contrive to know it. Man is a creature who not only knows, but who, being a self-conscious rather than a merely conscious agent, *knows that he knows*. When we know, we know that we know. Of course, much of what we take to be our knowledge may be incorrect. The problem of error is always with us. But if we are willing to suppose for the sake of argument and the inquiry that man is not totally deceived by all his knowledge, we can, I think, proceed with our theory of knowledge without being too much bothered by the fact that error occurs.

For another unfortunate characteristic of modern epistemological philosophy is the tendency to be too greatly influenced by the problem of error. Error occurs only in a real world. Man may misconceive the real, but he is never capable of perceiving the positively and completely unreal. If I say that I see pink elephants flying about in front of me, I can say so only because I live in a world in which there really are pink things, there really are elephants, and there really are birds that fly. Similarly, if I declare that Henry VIII had seven wives instead of six, citing in support of this contention some spurious and misleading item of historical evidence, the form of the judgement and its supposed basis is identical in both cases, and it is certainly true that Henry VIII did have a plurality of wives. Error always apes truth, and the theory of error is no more than a subtle refinement and qualification, a postscript added to the theory of knowledge. Even our erroneous judgements, in other words, belong to the same class as our correct judgements. How could we possibly know or discover that our erroneous judgements are erroneous except by contrasting them with other judgements that are certainly valid? The fact that error occurs, I would suggest, is not very relevant to the subtleties of epistemological theory. At all events, I propose to proceed in this chapter in the manner characteristic of ancient and medieval rather than of modern philosophy because, quite frankly, it seems to me the better way. First of all let us consider the kind of knowledge we do in fact possess and then let us inquire how it is that we attain it.

If history is knowledge of events located in past time, past time itself may be divided up into three areas or zones which are to some extent successive although to a certain significant degree they overlap. First of all there is an area of total darkness, an area in which the historians can see nothing for certain at all, or at all events only a very little, and these but faint, blurred outlines. The most obvious instance is the darkness of what is sometimes called pre-history, a lengthy period in which man left but little evidence of himself, and almost no evidence whatever of the events which occurred in the course of his existence. To some extent through archaeology, ethnology, and social anthropology, we know something of the forms and structures of social life in these primitive periods, but this is a knowledge of the context in which historical events occurred rather than a knowledge of the events them-selves. No doubt at these remote periods events occurred having the dramatic and personal character of the events with which we are familiar, but what they were and precisely how they occurred is necessarily hidden from our eyes.

Then, again, there are periods of historical twilight, to be distinguished from the darkness rather as in psycho-analysis the sub-conscious or pre-conscious is to be distinguished from the unconscious. These are areas of past time which are revealed to us, in so far as they are revealed to us at all, mainly by oral tradition, persisting for many centuries before it is written down, myths and legends, and customs which have survived so long that no one now knows precisely how they began or what they mean. Oral tradition and legend have rightly been treated by historians with a certain sceptical reserve, particularly by nineteenth-century historians, but these periods can also be examined to some extent by archaeo-logy, and during the last half-century or so archaeology has done a great deal to restore our faith in oral tradition and legend and the purely verbal memory transmitted from generation to generation among more or less illiterate peoples. Peoples who write little or nothing down tend to transmit oral material with much greater accuracy than people who are accustomed to leave written records of whatever they regard as worth remembering. This fact is important not only for biblical studies but for almost all early history. Thus there was a time when historians were sceptical as to whether the Trojan Wars of Homer ever occurred at all. Archaeology has demonstrated conclusively that they did. In the book of Genesis, Abraham behaves to Sarah and Hagar, both before and after the birth of Ishmael, in strict accord with the provisions of the Code of Hammurabi, despite the fact that these stories must have been orally transmitted for centuries by generations of people who had never so much as heard of the Code of Hammurabi.

The third area of past time we may call the area of historical daylight. In this area records and evidences of various kinds abound. They may sometimes conflict and lead the historian in different and incompatible directions, but in this area his chief difficulty is not that he cannot see, but rather that he can see too much. The area of historical daylight has a narrow rind which the historian can pierce to some extent with the aid of his own personal memory supplemented by that of his contemporaries. Thus Greek history in the classical period is very largely an autobiographical, anecdotal history of recent events. Thucydides himself had actually taken part in the Pelopponesian war, like the writers of the gospels in the New Testament. The so-called 'we' sections in the Acts of the Apostles in particular recall Thucydides, and, although much briefer, the introduction of St. Luke's Gospel is not unlike the first chapter of Thucydides' history. By contrast the historical sections of the Old Testament, with their many citations and quotations from already existing written documents, remind us of the procedure of modern rather than ancient Greek historians. 'Now the rest of the acts of King So-and-so, behold, they are written in the Book of the Chronicles of the Kings of Judah.' Similarly, Jeremiah dictated his oracles to a secretary, and no doubt these records were drawn upon by the later compiler of the Book of Jeremiah. The personal memories of the historian and his contemporaries are quickly exhausted, and after that we are dependent upon records bequeathed to us by people who have long passed away. Of course, even in the daylight there is a kind of darkness; there is no period of history about which we know everything. If I am face to face with my friend in the daylight I cannot see his back. It is always true that what we do not see is some kind of obverse of what we do see. The light, the darkness, and the twilight do to some extent overlap. There may, indeed, be a darkness in which there is no light, but there is no light in which there is no darkness, no shadow cast by the light itself.

In historical literature the term dark is more often used of the twilight periods than of the times of absolute darkness in which events are to us altogether invisible. Thus we speak of the European dark ages, meaning very roughly the period between the collapse of the Roman Empire in the west, say 411, and the coronation of Charlemagne in 800. I think people often fancy that the dark ages are called dark because this was a period in which particularly dark and dirty deeds were done. This is a total misapprehension of the term. Of course, dark and dirty deeds were committed in the dark ages, but, alas, deeds of this kind are common to all ages. From such a point of view we should have to say that the twentieth century, the century of Belsen and Dachau and the gas chambers of Auschwitz, is one of the darkest periods on record. No doubt these deeds were not darker or dirtier than many of those which were done before them, but at least they happened on a much larger scale. No, the dark ages are called dark simply because they are ages in which the historian cannot see very clearly.

However, they were not a period of total darkness; the historian can see to some extent. Hence I would prefer to call them twilight rather than dark ages. Thus I distinguish between real dark ages in which the historian cannot see at all, twilight ages in which his knowledge is meagre and uncertain, and daylight ages in which he can see clearly, although even here there occur the characteristic kinds of darkness which hedge around the circumference of light. Corresponding to this analysis is the distinction between totally unknown historical events, partly but meagrely-known historical events and well known, even if never quite totally known, historical events.

Now we have to consider a more subtle question. Are historical events perceived or are they always conjectured or intellectually reconstructed? Certainly a historical judgement is a verdict arrived at after an inspection of the evidence. Obviously no historical event is perceived by the historian himself. Let us consider a particular instance. 'King Charles was decapitated on January 30th, 1649.' Clearly, if this assertion is made by a contemporary historian writing some three hundred years later, he is delivering a verdict arrived at after some inspection of the evidence. Many people who were present testify to having seen the event with their own eyes; legal and state papers record it; and certainly no one appears to have met the ill-fated monarch subsequently. The events of the next decade all appear to take the sad king's fate for granted, so that no intelligible account of them could be given on the assumption that he somehow after all survived. Although the event was not itself perceived by the historian, it was certainly perceived by many of the authorities on whom the historian relies. In an instance like this we may properly speak of historical perception. When the historian asks the question *why* the unfortunate king met with this particular fate, he finds himself confronted with at least four possible answers, all of them well represented in the extant literature and all of them capable of reasonably convincing documentation: (1) Charles was beheaded as the more or less just consequence of political misgovernment and ineptitude as a statesman, a course of events in which the monarch's own personal weaknesses forced him to resort to a considerable amount of duplicity. (2) Charles died the death of a religious martyr and suffered as he did because of his championship of the Church against the vigorous protests of seventeenth-century puritans. (3) Charles represented a party upholding economic and sociological traditions based on semi-feudalism, and the agrarian, anti-capitalist social ethic of the medieval Church. This meant that he stood in the way of the new men and the strongest forces of social change, not necessarily of social progress, operating at the time. Charles, in other words, died because he was, in terms of the seventeenth-century current of events, an economic and social reactionary, and history swept him away. (4) Charles failed because he cravenly consented to the execution of Strafford, and thus lost the devoted services of the greatest politician and administrator of the time.

No doubt there is a grain of truth in all these theories; one overlaps the other. Thus, for example, Charles' forlorn attempt to govern without parliament and the new professional and commercial middle classes it represented was partly due to his religious fear that parliament would insist on attacking the Church. Here we may rightly say that the decision of any particular historian will be a matter of conjecture, determined at least to some extent by the kind of historian he is. If he is primarily a political historian he will probably give great weight to the first of our four verdicts. If he is primarily an ecclesiastical, religious and cultural historian he may lay his stress on the second. If he is primarily an economic historian he may be led to embrace the third. If he is primarily a kind of historical journalist, emphasizing personal matters like ability and statesmanlike know-how, he may be led to attach considerable importance to the execution of Strafford, and to the obverse factor represented by the adhesion of so able a man as Cromwell to the parliamentary cause. Probably, if he is a very good historian, he will not ignore the measure of truth contained in each of these verdicts, for none of them is altogether beside the mark. The historical verdict can never be simple.

A more Toynbean type of historian would presumably compare this episode to the many similar episodes to be found in human history; to the execution perhaps of Louis XVI, or to the loss of temporal power by Pius IX, or Britain's loss of the American colonies under George III. These instances would draw our attention to the fact that monarchy often suffers its worst reverses during the reigns of more than usually amiable and attractive monarchs. Ruthlessly efficient tyrants are rarely overthrown. Rather it is the hesitations and scruples of good and sensitive men in almost impossibly difficult circumstances that produce the collapse of such regimes. Louis XVI was decapitated, not Louis XIV; Charles, not Henry VIII; it is Pius IX who loses the temporal power, not Alexander VI, and so on. Ruthless men give life to strong monarchies. It is usually, I use the word in the literal sense, 'gentle men' who have the misfortune to suffer retribution for others' sins rather than their own. Charles, such a historian may well say, was too good a man to be tough enough to carry the burden of the Tudor inheritance in difficult and exacting times. Just so, to use a similar example of the same kind of process, twentieth-century Britain was too enlightened and democratic to bear any longer the responsibility of imperial power in India. Sometime, it would appear, behind a measure of historical failure there lies a certain degree of ethical success.

However, we persevere with our illustration too long. Our point is that whatever our verdict on this particular question, it will be an interpretative conjecture. To say that Charles the First was decapitated on January 30th, 1649, is very different from saying that this tragic event occurred justly because of his misgovernment, unjustly because of his religious faith, inevitably because of his agrarian economic and social sympathies, or accidentally because he made the mistake of 'dropping the pilot.' In the one case the historians can say, 'This is certainly what happened'; in the other case he must say, 'This in my view is the basic reason why it happened' or 'This seems to me the best available explanation of the event.' Clearly there must always be an important distinction between historical perception and historical conjecture, although any actual piece of historical writing will inevitably be a complex texture composed of both.

Yet we must not distinguish too sharply between the perception of sheer fact on the one hand and the conjectural interpretation of it on the other. A great deal of modern philosophy, particularly the kind that stems from the English empiricism of the eighteenth century, has been weakened by a concept of pure perception which does not correspond with any reality. First of all, we are taught, we perceive sense data, and we then proceed by conjectural interpretation to piece our sense data together into some kind of picture of an intelligible external world. The basic fallacy of eighteenth-century English empiricism was the idea that what we perceive directly consists of a large number of sense data, whereas it would seem very obvious to me that in fact we do not perceive sense data at all, but rather, through the channel and means provided by sense data, we directly perceive the world in which we are.

But whatever our view of this question a fallacy is involved whenever we suppose that human cognition consists of a primitive act of pure perception which is succeeded in time, no doubt in a blindingly short instant or fraction of time, by an act of conjectural interpretation. We may term this the fallacy of pure perception, and I want to say that in my view nothing of the kind ever occurs at all. Pure perception, if it occurred at all, would be a merely physiological act. Of course, we must agree that there is a physiology of perception, of vision or hearing as the case may be. Yet no knowledge of its physiological or neurological correlates can give any complete account of the act of perception. To suppose that it can rather resembles the error of the celebrated Dr. Kinsey who assumed that human sexuality is merely mammalian. In order to understand an act we must know not merely *what* is done, and *how* it is done, but also *who* does it. When the mammalian process occurs within the context of human personality, and as a moment in personal relationship, its nature must be entirely transformed. For everything that occurs within a context must to some extent at least be integrated within that context.

Precisely what perception is in the experience of the lower animals we do not know for certain, although some at least of its characteristics were successfully studied by the gestalt psychologists. But we do know that in the case of a human being, equipped with self-consciousness and memory, perception is never merely the perception of this or that but also the perception of this kind of thing and that kind of thing. It is never merely a perception of the object but also a perception of the meaning of the object; never merely this thing in itself, but also of its obvious analogies to the other things. This is because in the case of human beings the very act of perception tends to verbalize it. If, for example, I perceive a crocodile at the zoo, I perceive it not merely as this particular crocodile, but also as one of the crocodiles. Possibly I have seen other crocodiles or at least pictures of them, or I have read descriptions of the crocodile and have at least some knowledge of its characteristics. I recognize at once that this is one of the crocodiles. In those instances in which a man does perceive something which he is totally unable to place, he is immediately troubled intellectually, and even then invents a category into which the object will fit, a category of the mysterious, a broad category hospitably comprehending all the things which he cannot understand. In other words, human perception is always perception of meaning as well as of sheer physical factuality. It always arranges things in categories or significant classes in the very act of perceiving. We may say that this also is an instance of what we have called typology. The ability to arrange experiences typologically is thus characteristic not merely of the intellectual disciplines that discover meaning in scripture or in history, but of the whole range of human experience. The perception of meaning is not subsequent to the recognition of physical fact but coincidental with it. Pure perception, the mere apprehension of totally uninterpreted physical actualities, is an abstraction which, so far as human beings are concerned, is never known to occur

Now, of course, we know well enough, once we reach the point of metaphysical analysis and speculation, that in fact there must always be a margin of error in this process. Everything is not merely an instance of some general type or kind of thing; everything is also itself. Some degree of uniqueness characterizes everything that is. Indeed, uniqueness in my view is the proper theme of metaphysics. It is perhaps more generally supposed that the proper theme of metaphysics is the transcendental, but this I believe is an error. Given, for example, a polytheistic account of the transcendental, a fellowship of gods coinhabiting some ultimate and olympian heaven, it is quite possible for a classical writer like Cicero to write a treatise on the divine nature, which the gods are supposed to share in common, that is not in any sense metaphysical. It is monotheism which inevitably transforms theology into metaphysics, for metaphysics is above everything else the form of thought which endeavours to grasp and interpret the reality of the unique.

All this is brought out very clearly in the Christological discussions of the early Church. Christ is man. He shares with human beings all the characteristics that they share with each other. In this sense he is indeed one of the men, but like every man that ever was, Christ has also his own uniqueness, his personality, that which he shares with no other man whatsoever. The uniqueness of Christ is the uniqueness of God. His human nature is the human nature of the divine person, and his divine person is the divine person in the human nature. This metaphysical Christology of the fathers and councils is not only the culmination, the supreme achievement, of the philosophical genius of the classical world, it is also the beginning of modern philosophy. Our academic institutions somehow contrive to provide courses in the history of western philosophy which take no notice at all of the development of patristic theology, and often very little notice of medieval thought either, although with regard to this latter the situation is rapidly improving. I am quite sure that no very discerning or accurate account of modern western philosophy can possibly be given if we omit so many of modern philosophy's foundations. To take but one example, the terms *person* and *nature*, as more and more sharply defined by the fathers of the fourth and fifth centuries, in order to fit them for the purposes of Christological discussion and definition, strongly resemble the use of the terms *existence* and *essence* in modern existentialism. It would not be altogether fanciful to say that the Christological discussions of the patristic period constitute the first, and still perhaps the best and the sanest, essays in existentialist analysis. Nowadays, of course, we have rather psychologized the term personality, closely affiliating and linking it with words like disposition, character and temperament. It is well to remember that originally, when first employed in intellectual and philosophical discussion, it was a purely metaphysical word, referring to the uniqueness of each particular human being. Later it was to become an axiological term, and it was declared that personality is the highest and noblest thing that God has made, but as a psychological term it is clearly something of a failure, and psychologists should certainly be encouraged to invent some other word for their own proper purposes.

Outside metaphysics, however, and clearly history must exist outside metaphysics, the clue to meaning is the arrangement and classification of things in terms of the types or kinds which they embody or to which they conform. Experience becomes significant to us, that is, it becomes true human experience, at the moment in which we can look *at* something or other and say to ourselves, in effect, 'This is one of those.' Of course, we know that each particular thing is a unique variation of the universal theme, which it presents in its own peculiar way, but nevertheless, the recognition of meaning comes when we are able to distinguish the theme of which it is a variation. It is perhaps in this sense that the typological mode of biblical interpretation and the Toynbean kind of history shows itself as continuous with science and, indeed, with all human experience. Experience is meaningful because it occurs in a world characterized by a subtle kind of recurrence, a stream of events metaphysically distinct from each other, and yet constantly presenting us with reminiscences of pattern and structure, with many distinct kinds of analogy, so that again and again we can say to ourselves, 'We have been here before.' That is never the whole truth, of course, but it is one part or aspect of the truth. Experience is meaningful not merely because it occurs in this kind of a world, but because it occurs for beings equipped with memory and that plastic eye for function and structure which enables us at least in rough and ready fashion to distinguish between that in the thing which affiliates it with other things and those more inscrutable characteristics which are peculiar to itself.

Thus whether we are thinking of physical nature or human history every act of perception is at least pregnant with elements of interpretation. The role of the historical thinker is to continue in a disciplined, sophisticated way the element of interpretation to be found in the immediate experience of the event. No doubt thought will refine the spontaneous interpretation, sometimes it may even correct it, but at least the interpreter is not adding to the experience of the event an element entirely unwarranted and unheralded by it.

The point may be illustrated by a famous theological controversy. It was rather fashionable to suppose forty or fifty years ago, indeed, the impression still lingers here and there even now, that the Christological thought of the early Church is quite remote from and alien to the New Testament. The New Testament was supposed to set before us a pure Jesus of history, whereas the early Church builds up a concept of the Christ of Faith. There were even some people who proposed that we should abandon the intellectual treasure of the concept in order to enjoy once more the warm immediacy of the pure percept. But if we turn to the New Testament we shall see at once that this was not and could not have been the case. In fact, the first apprehension of Jesus filled men's minds with the possibilities of staggering interpretations. The New Testament is saturated by the thought of the earliest Church, demanded from it and forced out of it by the tremendous impact of the personality of Christ. No doubt the subsequent work of the early Church refined and deepened this thought by an intellectualism which was a genuine spirituality and a spirituality which took the form of a profound intellectualism. But it was only continuing what the New Testament itself had begun and carrying it to a conclusion which the spirit implicit in the New Testament could not but approve.

Thus in all experience, in the transition from empirical immediacy to reflective comprehension, the movement is not from pure perception to intellectual interpretation, but from primitive perception which is still primarily the perception of meaning to an interpretation which articulates all that was latent and implicit in that first primary perception. Even perception is an intellectual act, because it is perception by an intellectual being. To think of it as mere sensation is to misunderstand precisely what it is that happens when sensation occurs within the context of self-conscious personality. Our sensations are not merely sensations; they are always the sensations of intellectual beings. In evolution every new development, each new grade or type of being, takes into itself all that went before it and lies beneath it, but only at the cost of integrating all that went before and lies beneath it with the new sovereign principle of its own being. There is much in man which we see to be very similar to what we find in the animals, but in man it is in a new context and therefore in man its nature and function is transformed.

I conclude from this discussion that all perception, even its most primitive levels, is a perception of meaning or of events pregnant with meaning, precisely because all human perception is an activity of intellectual beings, and takes place in an intellectual context. Historical interpretation, as distinct from primary historical perception, is thus always an extending, a refining, a deepening of an element given in and with and by the primary experience, or, to put it another way, historical thinking is radically continuous with historical experience, for all experience is experience of meaning. History considered as process, as observed flow of events, is thus 'oven-ready' for history considered as reflective interpretation, made for it, so to speak, evoking it, demanding and at last securing it. Just so the New Testament is 'oven-ready' for the theological speculations of the early Church. If we have the one, then sooner or later we must have the other, reality being what it is and man being what he is. Just as, sooner or later, nature must beget science, so events must beget history, and God must beget theology. There is no escaping the inevitable transition; there is no frustrating these intellectual necessities.

The doctrine that I have thus briefly outlined seems to me to have two consequences important in the present discussion. In the first place this insistence that all historical experience is the experience of meaning, that there is no more any pure perception in history than anywhere else, that all experience is continuous with, indeed, the first phase of, interpretative thought, means that positivist views of history, like positivist views of nature and science, must be absolutely rejected. All positivism is built on an artificial and abstract notion of pure experience, to which nothing in actual human experience corresponds. First the senses give us the experiences and then the intellect devises ways of relating them. I do not believe for one moment that this corresponds with the facts. It would be nearer to the truth to say that first the sensible mode of experience gives us our primitive contacts with meaning, and that our subsequent intellectual experience refines and relates them into some more profound intellectual system. At all events, if what I have said is true, no positivistic or purely behaviourist narrative of uninterpreted historical facts is conceivable. We do not experience things in that way, and we cannot narrate things in that way. All historical experience is experience of meaning; all historical research is an exploration of meaning; all historical narration is an exposition of meaning. We can deny that this is so, but we cannot do or write anything which does not in some way or other imply that it is so.

Even if we were to conclude that all life and history is meaningless, this would, after all, be its meaning, a meaning which has inspired many existentialist philosophers, writers and poets to the composition of many books, some of them good ones. To say that the doctrine that life and history are meaningless is nevertheless to ascribe to life and history a meaning sounds somewhat paradoxical at first, but if it is possible for the psychiatrist to give us a rational account of insanity, it should be possible for an imaginative philosopher to find in the alleged meaninglessness of life and experience the clue to its ultimate meaning. Of course, I do not myself agree with this kind of philosopher, but I would say that we cannot escape from the meaning of life and historical existence merely by declaring it to be meaningless, for even this meaninglessness will turn into a peculiar kind of meaning.

What really makes any kind of positivism impossible is the fact that we are human beings. A purely positivist, behaviourist account of life and existence might perhaps be given by one of the lower animals, except, of course, that the lower animals never give any account of life and existence at all. We do not know too much about the way in which the animal experiences life, about what he finds in life, but we know enough to say that if he were a philosopher his experience might very well make him a positivist. It would certainly make him a nominalist, for he has no words at all, and having no words is not so different from having words and finding most of them, and almost all of our more intelligent ways of using them, meaningless. It is rather like the contrast between the genuine savage and the sophisticated, back-to-nature man who reverts to savagery from civilization. The one is what he is with dignity; the other pretends to be what he is not with absurdity. If the animal were to be a positivist and a nominalist, I should be inclined to excuse him, for probably all his experience of life points in that direction. The human being who takes this point of view I regard as a rather more perverse phenomenon. For *our* experience of life points in a very different direction. Our experience of life is an experience of meaning and an experience of the power and vitality of the word. If it is through the Word of God that the cosmos was created, it is similarly through the words of science that the cosmos is rendered intelligible. If the Word was made flesh, that was only possible because in man the flesh had already through the long processes of evolution been made word. If for us even meaninglessness inevitably turns into a kind of meaning, that is only because, just as the leopard cannot change his spots, even so man remains essentially and inescapably the bearer and expositor of the meanings he finds himself compelled by his nature to recognize, and by which he finds himself surrounded on every side of his existence.

In traditional Christian thought—I have in mind particularly St. Augustine and his followers—the problems of epistemology are handled in terms of the doctrine of man, of man as a being made in the image of God the creator. It is because of man's remote but nevertheless real kinship with the Creator that he is able to make sense of the creation, that the creation is not merely apparent to him but also meaningful to him. St. Augustine and his followers are fundamentally platonists, with the result that this theory is first conceived and thought out with reference to the mathematical characteristics of the universe, and hence with what we should now call mathematical physics primarily in mind. It is a mistake to suppose that the philosophy and physics of the middle ages were so entirely Aristotelian as the seventeenth century, in the heat of its reaction against later medieval thought, too emphatically believed and alleged. One consequence of taking the violence of the Renaissance and seventeenth-century reaction against medieval thought too seriously is that we lose the thread of continuity that runs through all history, and even fall into the habit of supposing that the post-Renaissance thinkers made a kind of new start without any reference to what went before. The truth is that through the middle ages the Augustinian tradition maintained itself as a sustained protest against the Aristotelianism of the later medieval period, and that it was from this tradition that the early modern thinkers and scientists stem.

Thus, according to Galileo, 'mathematics is the language in which the book of nature is written.' For him the really astonishing thing was that man should be able to speak the language in which the book of nature is written. The sub-human creatures consort with nature, are reared and developed in the context of nature, just as much as men, but they never learn to speak nature's language. Galileo's solution of the problem is straight out of Augustine. Man can speak the language in which the book of nature is written, or is at least capable of learning that language, because man is made in the image of, is, indeed, the child, however disobedient a child, of the Creator of nature. Galileo's solution of his problem can be paralleled again and again from St. Augustine himself, and in other Augustinians like St. Bonaventura, who is much less interested in the mathematics of the subject, or Grosseteste, who is much more concerned with the problems of physics. Thus epistemology for all these thinkers is a kind of footnote or postscript to what we may call the ontology of man.

As I have already hinted, in epistemology the proper order of procedure is this: First we must know, then we must know that we know, and last of all we must inquire how it is that we know what we know. Inevitably when the problems of epistemology are discussed from this point of view the problem of knowledge becomes one aspect of the doctrine of man's status in the universe, of man's place in the order of reality. Man alone among the creatures that we find in the world is an inveterate knower, and this is interpreted as characteristic of the peculiar kind of being which he inherits.

It is one of the paradoxes of the history of thought that Plato, who was so much less interested in what we should now call the problems of science than Aristotle, is nevertheless much closer to the spirit of modern science than his peripatetic successor. In fact, the structure of modern mathematical physics is fundamentally platonic in spirit. There is a world in which we live and perceive, and a world of mathematical ideas in which we think and conceive. The more profoundly we enter intellectually into the depths of this latter world, the more we are able to comprehend and handle the problems arising from our intercourse with actual things in the perceptual world. Our intercourse with the world of ideas enhances and extends the area and depth of our dominion over the world of things. How this is possible is indeed a problem, and the fact that it is possible sheds a flood of light on the nature and potentialities, the status in the realm of being, of those creatures for whom it is possible.

There are perhaps three basic types of epistemology known to western philosophy:

1. The platonic, theistic, Christian type of epistemology which I have briefly described. Man is capable of scientific and philosophical knowledge because his mind is akin to that of the world's Creator. So that the act of human understanding, when it comprehends, is a kind of mystical act in which the creature participates to some small extent in the operations of the divine mind.

2. The categorical idealism of Kant and his successors. According to this doctrine man understands the world of his immediate experience because in the very act of experiencing it he has assimilated it, even subdued it, to the forms of his understanding.

3. Naturalistic epistemology, according to which man can understand the world merely because he has lived with it for a long time, and the world itself has presided over the evolution and growth of the forms and devices which he employs in his quest for understanding.

The third is perhaps the weakest of these three doctrines, because it fails to see that between the perceptual world of man's immediate experience and the conceptual world in terms of which he understands his immediate experience there lies a great gulf which can be bridged only by a prolonged process of deliberate abstraction from his immediate experience, or by the use of analogy, or by a combination of both abstraction and analogy. The abstract and conceptual account of our world provided by scientific theory in no way resembles the world we know immediately in perceptual experience, and is indeed discontinuous with it.

In practice, the general, and inevitable, tendency of such a naturalistic epistemology is towards some kind of phenomenalistic and positivist account of science, according to which science merely observes recurrences, rhythms and periodicities in immediately observed phenomena, and proceeds to invent techniques for formulating these phenomenal relationships and thus predicting their future course. I believe that this is an incorrect account of what happens in science and a misapprehension of its real achievement. We have only to consider the most advanced of our sciences, mathematical physics, in order to perceive its extraordinary inadequacies.

The second, Kantian, type of epistemology really implies that even when he thinks himself to be understanding the world man really only understands himself, and the strange operations of the pure reason. We know what the world appears to be like when man experiences it, but we never know what it is like in and for itself. Scientific knowledge is a knowledge of phenomena categorically organized, although oddly enough the categories in terms of which we organize this knowledge of phenomena are not themselves included among the phenomena, nor are they implied by the phenomena, nor could they be deduced or induced from the phenomena. It is a strange amalgam of Augustinian doctrines minus God, and of the empiricist account of experience minus those endemic limitations of empiricism so decisively demonstrated by Hume.

In my view Platonism as baptized by St. Augustine still holds the field. For this is not an epistemological theory merely devised in order to get us out of an epistemological difficulty. This is basically an ontological interpretation of man which proves to have the subsequent advantage of solving also our epistemological problems.

But if, since Galileo, mathematical physics has seemed to be the most striking example of the power and validity of the Augustinian doctrine, it is by no means the only application of it. Thus in St. Bonaventura we have an elaborate development of the idea of a symbolical universe in which all things speak to man of God and nothing is ultimately meaningless. No doubt this doctrine, particularly when unpurged and uncriticized by any strong tradition of scientific thought, led to many fanciful and imaginative refinements, provided an overwhelming temptation to merely whimsical minds, but certainly it moved in the direction of our doctrine that events are intrinsically meaningful.

In the nineteenth century we find similar developments in Dilthey's philosophy of history. Dilthey is opposed to the kind of philosophical reformulation of history to be found in writers like Hegel and Compte, and to that extent this book is close to his point of view. Yet for him also historical thought is essentially an appreciation of meaning. Dilthey is close also to Vico, the great eighteenth-century Italian philosopher. For Vico, to know and understand something is the same thing as to have made it. Men have made history and therefore men can understand it because of their ability to enter sympathetically into each other's states of mind and purposes. According to Dilthey, historical understanding (*das Verstehen*) is essentially a way of entering into the thoughts and intentions of men which is characteristically human. For him 'lived experience is, of its own nature, instinct with form and meaning.'[1] 'The significance which the fact acquires,' he says, 'as the determination imparted by a meaningful whole to its parts is a living connection and not an intellectual relation, not an insertion of reason or thought into that part of the process. Significance is extracted from life itself.'[2] Of course, Dilthey is too post-Kantian, too much a man of the nineteenth century, to introduce theology into his thought. Men have made history, and therefore man can enter into it and understand it in terms of human feeling. By insisting on the role of man he short-circuits the role of God. But he only does this at a heavy cost, for now, in him as in Vico, the role of understanding in history in this special sense (*das Verstehen*) is what distinguishes history from the natural sciences; but we have already insisted, following Galileo and the Augustinians, that in this matter there is a very important analogy between history and the natural sciences, at all events when a natural science is developed to maturity, as in the case of modern mathematical physics.

One of our main difficulties in the realm of the philosophy of science is due to the fact that so many of the

---

[1] Quoted from H. A. Hodges' *Philosophy of Wilhelm Dilthey*. Routledge & Kegan Paul, London, 1952, p. 150.   [2] Ibid., p. 150 f.

natural sciences have either not reached this degree of maturity, or arrived at it only very recently, so that the philosophy of science from the seventeenth century to the present time has been too greatly influenced by the procedure of non-mature sciences, still too much taken up with the merely empirical collection, inspection and classification of their proper data. This has made possible the widespread notion that natural science is merely empirical. It is only when the point is reached at which it becomes clear that the business end of science is the interpretation of data in terms of mathematically conceived theories that a merely empirical understanding of the scientific process begins to break down.

If, in fact, there is something analogous to Dilthey's *das Verstehen* even in mathematical physics, then the mere account of it in terms of man's intuitive understanding of man will not do. In any case the Augustinian would insist that human feeling affiliates man to God as well as man to man, because man is made in God's image. Of course, the dangers of anthropomorphism are very great here, and must be carefully guarded against; but the dangers of anthropomorphism are only as great as they are in Christian and biblical thought because at least a certain qualified degree of anthropomorphism is valid, once the doctrine has been accepted that man is made in God's image. Dilthey, in other words, only evicts God from his system of historical thought at the cost of snapping the thin, fine thread of continuity that links the historical with the natural sciences. Of course, we must distinguish the historical from the natural sciences, but it is better not to make the distinction too absolutely. At all events from the Augustinian point of view maintained here, God, the author of the historical drama, is also the creator of the natural process. The extraordinary thing about man is that he is equipped with a capacity to enter into and comprehend both the natural process and the historical drama, and this despite the manifest differences between the two and the very different ways in which he is related to them.

Of course, for the Christian thinker the final verification of this thesis and the supreme exemplification of it is to be found in the fact of the Incarnation. Man is such that God can become man without ceasing to be God. That eternally present in the Godhead, in the image of which man is made, can enter into and participate in the drama of human existence. Indeed, the Christ is that point in time, the fullness of time, upon which the whole drama hinges. From the Christian point of view the evolution of man culminates in what theologians call the hypostatic union, in the figure of the God-Man, the divine person in the context of the human nature, and the human nature in the possession of the divine person. It is at that point that the Christian sees both what God is and what man is. Man is made to be God's and God makes himself to be man. Both the theological and the anthropological implications of this event are staggering. There is a consanguinity, a reciprocity between God and man which prompts at the same time both an exalted humanism, as we consider the magnificence of man's calling and destiny, and a profound humility as we are sobered by the thought of the heavy responsibilities born by so magnificent a creature. But at least it ceases, from such a point of view, to be a problem that man is able to enter into the meaning of nature and history, for now all meaning is seen to be God's meaning. The meaningless is non-existent, and all meaning is seen to be at least in principle within our human grasp, there for our taking. So that such meaning as we find in the events around us is no longer the meaning which we give to them, but rather the meaning which we find in them, which through them God presents to us.

Chapter 6

THE ONTOLOGY OF HISTORY

W E now turn to the metaphysical account of the status of the historical drama in the order and scale of reality. I use the term historical drama rather than the more familiar phrase the historical process because there is a sense in which drama and process are antithetical. Processes occur in nature. A process properly speaking is a procession of functionally, and perhaps causally, related impersonals. Drama, on the other hand, is always concerned with the clash and confrontation, the union and amity, the antagonism, and enmity of personalities. Primitive man has a habit of dramatizing in his myths the impersonal natural processes. Sophisticated modern man is more inclined to depersonalize even the drama in which he himself is engulfed, by turning biology into physics, by transmuting existence into psychology, by conceiving history as economics. Of the two philosophical errors ours is no doubt the greater. Primitive mythology with its so-called pathetic fallacy of personalizing the impersonal is, after all, no more than a dubious and perhaps rather forlorn speculation. Our modern apathetic fallacy is an almost wilful misperception and misconception of a plain reality that stares us in the face. The personal cannot be depersonalized without doing violence to the most obvious of facts.

Of course, it is true that history does include and contain trends of development which can be intellectually abstracted from concrete history and treated as processes. The most obvious of these elements is that kind of economic process which binds and relates together multitudes of people scattered all over the globe who never actually meet each other as persons at all. These are sometimes described by the sociologists as the 'secondary associations,' and it is certainly possible to give a clear, if somewhat abstract, account of such things in impersonal process language. However, history considered as a whole is personal drama, and to consider the ontological characteristics of history as such is merely one way of scrutinizing the ontological characteristics of personality as such.

Here I shall be considering the account of history which is provided by Christian and biblical thought, for in the last resort it is that account of history which is given by the mind which has accepted the biblical revelation which really makes sense of the view that history is such that revelation can be given from within it. Or, to put it another way, it is the success of this Christian and biblical account of history considered simply as a penetrating interpretation of history, which verifies or goes far towards verifying, our initial hypothesis that history is such that revelation can occur.

In order to provide this account, I shall call upon four basic categories of Christian thought: sin, eschatology, the tension between eternity and time, and freedom.

I. SIN

The category of sin differs from that of evil, or the pain which so troubles the sensitive conscience, or perhaps nerves, of the utilitarian philosopher, because of its Godward reference. Categories like pain and evil are concerned with regrettable and undesirable actualities in so far as they damage and distort our human experience of life and our human conduct of affairs. Sin is no doubt a way of getting at the same actualities, but the term refers to what these things are for and before God rather than simply to their effect on us. Sin, we may say, is evil considered in its Godward rather than in its manward aspect. Sin is a purely theological category. To confront evil as sin is to evoke the idea of God.

For the utilitarian and many other non-theological thinkers, evil, interpreted primarily as pain, is a great philosophical problem, perhaps above all others the problem which estranges such minds from any belief in God. Certainly the Christian theist is driven to admit that God is neither hedonist nor utilitarian. He does not regard pain as the worst of all things, nor is he so horrified by the consciousness that his universe includes pain as to will that the experiment of creation should be brought to an end. To put it crudely, the Christian is bound to admit that God is not squeamish. On the other hand, he is not bound to admit, indeed, cannot admit, that God directly wills or causes pain. Too many modern philosophers seem to take it for granted that a more or less Calvinistic idea of God, as the Sovereign Will who ordains everything that happens, is the only possible interpretation of the divine omnipotence. They cannot conceive of the omnipotent God who creates a universe characterized by various degrees of spontaneity and freedom, still less a God who subsequently respects what he has created. For them, apparently, if God creates anything at all it can only be a kind of cosmic puppet show, in which nothing happens at all except when God pulls the strings.

What the people who are so quick to ask why so much evil and pain occurs in a world created by an omnipotent God of justice and love are really asking is; 'Why did not God prefer to create a cosmic machine for the automatic production of righteousness?' They fail to consider that this merely automatic righteousness would not really be righteousness at all, and to take into sufficient account the possibility that God might very well say, for reasons which even men can discover and echo, that what he has created is infinitely better than any conceivable machine for the automatic ejection of righteousness, with happiness and sanctity mass-produced like sausages.

After all this is not very surprising. For the most part philosophy is thought and written by intellectuals, and intellectuals tend notoriously to be hyper-sensitive where physical and psychic pain are concerned, so that the view that pain is the worst of all things comes very easily to their minds. Nor is this hyper-sensitivity by any means an altogether undesirable thing in itself. It is the rationalization of it into various brands of utilitarian philosophy that is so one-sided and defective. Surely the intellect of the true intellectual should be sufficiently objective, self-forgetful and humble to assure him that the intellectual is not the only kind of man, nor even necessarily the best kind.

The Christian will say that if God tolerates the existence of pain and evil in his universe he also wills to share it, and of this the Cross is the supreme symbol. If he expects us to endure these things he never expects us to endure them alone. There are, in fact, two problems of pain. There is the purely theoretical problem for theodicy raised by the utilitarian philosopher, and there is the existential problem of pain raised by Christianity. The existential problem is not the problem of how to interpret and explain the presence of pain and evil in the good God's world; rather it is the problem of how so to bear and endure pain that faith is not turned into doubt, hope into despair, and charity extinguished in bitterness and hate. It is this second, existential problem of pain that is solved so triumphantly by Christ on the Cross, and, of course, in those many martyrdoms which participate in the reality of Calvary.

Historically the idea of pain in God has sometimes been called, and has sometimes deserved to be called, the patripassian heresy. God, it has been said, cannot have anything imposed or inflicted upon him from sources external to himself. All pain, it has been supposed, is imposed or inflicted by another, and therefore the idea of pain in God is unthinkable. But we may very well question whether it is necessarily true that all pain must be imposed or inflicted upon us by some agent external to the self. On the contrary, there are some kinds of pain which we only experience because we are what we are, kinds of pain which are not inflicted upon the self but rather express the self. Then also there are types of pain which we deliberately will to share with others even though we could escape them. In other words, there can be a conception of pain in God which avoids the patripassian heresy. God's pain is the expression and inevitable by-product of his love. He is not the less but the more the sovereign of the universe in experiencing it, nor need we suppose that God's pain in contemplating and sharing the pain of creation in any way abates his joy.

In any case pain, from the standpoint of the Christian philosopher, is only one species of evil. We may define pain as physical and psychic evil and put it side by side with other types of evil, such as aesthetic evil (ugliness), intellectual evil (error), social evil (injustice), and moral evil (unrighteousness). These are all evil in their own fashion and degree, and any survey of the so-called problem of evil must necessarily take them all into account.

For Christianity sin has a history but no metaphysics. This is the real significance of the doctrine of the fall. Sin belongs to time; it is one of those things that has had a beginning and therefore must have an end. The very word 'fall' means that sin is a historical accident. Some contemporary theologians, having grown sceptical about the historicity of the fall story in the Bible, proceed, in a manner scandalously out of harmony with the Christian tradition, to supply sin with a metaphysic and deny it a history. Sin is now commonly represented as an almost inevitable ingredient in finite personality, so that we might say, from this point of view, that to create finite persons is inevitably to create sinners. This is a doctrine, however, to which, as we have said, the whole Christian tradition is opposed. The early Christian thinkers arrived at the doctrine of the fall not merely because it seemed to them, following St. Paul, that there was a fall-story in scripture, but also because they were concerned to reject two other explanations of the fact of sin which were radically out of harmony with the biblical doctrine of God as supremely powerful and utterly righteous.

The first of these was dualism. According to this doctrine God is not supremely powerful. Indeed, his supremacy is threatened by the existence of an ultimate principal of evil in all things antithetical to the God of righteousness. The universe is partly created by the God of righteousness and partly created by the ultimate principle of all evil. Usually in these so-called Manichean heresies the portion of the creation attributed to the ultimate principle of evil was the material portion, but of course, this could conceivably be located elsewhere (e.g. in the fact of created finitude) without destroying the theory. In Christian mythology and imagery the ultimate principle of evil is transformed into the devil. But the devil is a created agent—Lucifer, the sun of the morning, a perverted being who, despite all his perversions, remains inherently good, and who, since he is a creature, is not really ultimate at all. In Christianity none is ultimate but God. This Manichean view somewhat resembles Plato's doctrine in the *Timaeus*. The creation is mixed, being compounded of a brutish necessity that resists the purposes of God and a righteous freedom that fulfils them. The non-dualistic view which Christian thinkers were also concerned to repudiate is simply that God himself has created those elements in the universe which lead inevitably to evil, so that both good and evil are equally works of the one God.

If, then, we feel compelled to reject both these views, the only alternative is the belief that sin and evil are somehow accidental, actual but not fated by-products of that spontaneity and freedom and momentum of its own which God has imparted to his creation. According to this view sin is something which happens in the created temporal order but has no ground, repercussions, or consequences in the eternal, divine order. Sin and its consequences have historical actuality, but no ultimate standing or being of their own. In the technical sense sin is nothing, it is the absence of good rather than the presence of something absolutely non-good.

This is the so-called deprivatory theory of evil which we find in St. Augustine and the classical theologians, and which has been so much misunderstood by many modern theologians. It is important to remember that this view declares sin to be unreal in a special metaphysical sense of the word unreal. Of course, it is not an absurd doctrine which denies the historical actuality of sin. On the contrary, according to this doctrine, historical actuality is about all that sin has. What it denies is that there can be any metaphysics of sin, any grounding of this proximate historical actuality in ultimate being. Indeed, it is this doctrine which prevents the Christian thinker from identifying immediate historical actuality with ultimate being. This is the Christian philosopher's characteristic way of embodying in his own formulations the distinction between appearance and reality so characteristic of many classical philosophers and by no means entirely outgrown even yet. Usually the distinction, developed along Platonic lines, takes the form of an antithesis between appearance as manifested to the senses and reality as thought by the intellect. (We have already noticed an echo of this Platonic motif in contemporary mathematical physics.) This way of stating the distinction between appearance and reality is rejected by the Christian religion. God is the creator of all things visible and invisible, with the consequence that both the sensible experience which acquaints us with the visible and the intellectual experience which acquaints us with the intelligible are valid ways of experiencing which bring us into contact with genuine reality. God has so created the world that neither the senses nor the intellect are altogether misled.

Nevertheless, even in Christianity, one great distinction remains, the distinction between temporal historical actuality and eternal divine reality. It is the element of sin in the former which threatens to mislead us about the character of the latter. Sin belongs to time and history alone and has no counterpart in the eternal divine reality. It is metaphysically non-significant. Yet even in saying this we must once more distinguish. Sin as accomplished fact is metaphysically insignificant, yet man's capacity to sin, the possibility of his engaging in a course of becoming which frustrates and negates his true being, is very significant indeed from the point of view of what we may call the metaphysics of man. Though the sin itself is metaphysically insignificant, the fact that man is capable of being a sinner, of having a becoming which does not match his being, is metaphysically very significant indeed. For it is, after all, a very peculiar kind of being who can conceivably have a temporal becoming and historical actuality which does not reflect his ontological character. To say that sin is in history and peculiar to history, indeed, a historical accident, is to set up a schism between being and becoming, a possibility of unreality, a mode of not-being, the biblical *vanity*,[1] which tells us not a little about created being itself.

[1] In the Bible the words 'vain' and 'vanity' always connote the idea of emptiness, fruitlessness or worthlessness, never conceit. Cf. the use of the term throughout the Book of Ecclesiastes.

Man knows and experiences what he calls his freedom primarily as freewill or freedom of decision and choice. The danger of considering freedom only in these terms is that the evil decision or choice appears to be just as characteristic an act of freedom as the righteous decision or choice. It is thus that we are so often betrayed into the use of dualistic language about the struggle between good and evil, as though these were two equal but antithetical powers. Such language is foreign to the best traditions of Christian thought. For Christianity, the righteous choice is free (i.e. participates in, reflects, is instrumental to the free purposes of God) in a way in which the evil choice never is. The evil choice involves a submission to the currents of perversion running all through the process of historical actuality, whereas the righteous choice submits only to the eternal righteousness of God. The righteous choice, we may say, although made in time and history, really belongs to eternity, whereas the evil choice belongs only to history. History from this point of view is thus that sphere of being in which evil is possible. All evil is temporal and historical. Evil is inconceivable in any other setting. By accident, therefore, history has become the one locus of evil.

It is for this reason that Christian thought assigns to sin an origin in time called the Fall. Of course, the origins of sin belong in the sense of our history A to pre-history rather than to recorded or recordable history itself, and therefore have to be interpreted in mythological rather than in historical terms. Here we come to another problem of the Christian thinker as he confronts scripture. The Old Testament does not include any myth dealing merely with the origins of sin. The nearest to it is the story about the fallen angels consorting with the daughters of men in Genesis 6, according to which all subsequent human generations inherit corruption from the fallen angels. In fact, Christian thought has made little or no use of this particular myth, although St. Paul quaintly refers to it in suggesting that it is better for women to veil their charms in church. The Tower of Babel story is after all primarily a myth about the origin of the various languages spoken by different groups of the human race, and the Garden of Eden story is very clearly intended primarily as an 'origin of work' story rather than as an 'origin of sin' story.

The Genesis myth of Adam and Eve in the Garden of Eden is, of course, not historical, but many commentators have failed to observe that, although in no sense reliable history, it is quite excellent from the point of view of social anthropology. Adam and Eve are depicted as naked, food-gathering savages, living an undemanding, idle life in a fertile jungle, where food comes easily and the climate is neither rigorous nor exacting. The economic condition of the first human beings is thus remarkably similar to that of the great apes, for example, the gorillas and the chimpanzees. This fits in with all that we are compelled to conjecture about human origins. The food-gathering stage is the simplest possible human condition, an economy continuous with that of man's sub-human ancestors. This, in fact, is how man must have started. The story goes on to narrate how man left the garden and, in a less clement habitat, found that he could live only by work. This is the origin of agriculture rather than the origin of sin. Nevertheless, the transition from food-gathering to agriculture, from innocent, happy idleness to working by the sweat of the brow, is connected in the myth with the loss of innocence. We may well conjecture that there must have been some point of dawning knowledge in time at which man failed to make the leap from passive, idle, animal innocence to deliberate willed righteousness, a point at which men at last grew conscious of and knew themselves and yet failed to will to be themselves, but rather willed that they might become whatever they might will to become. It was at the point at which, through dawning self-knowledge, this leap from innocence to righteousness became necessary that man stumbled and fell short, with consequences which could not but affect and influence all future generations. Obviously the actual episodes in which this grave event occurred belongs to pre-history and are hidden from our gaze, like the origin of so many human things and institutions, but I believe the theory that sin must have had such a tragic historical origin is still very much the best one, and from the anthropological point of view still very much the most probable.

The fact that sin was possible is too often and too easily interpreted as a mere consequence of human freedom considered as freedom of decision or choice. We must realize that even in the sub-human creation there exist analogies to freedom, just as we find among the animals analogies to intelligence. It is as though in all evolution there are currents in the direction which ultimately formulates itself as man. It is fatal to interpret man in terms of evolution if we never attempt to interpret evolution in terms of man. Perhaps the widespread welcome to Pierre Teilhard de Chardin's book *The Phenomenon of Man*,[1] is due to the fact that he has at long last very clearly interpreted evolution in terms of man, and seen in man the clue to our understanding of the evolutionary process. Thus we find that everywhere things have a spontaneity, a momentum and intractability of their own which is analogous to what we know as self-conscious freedom in man. The sub-human things, we may say, obstinately insist on being themselves, but man in history is a being who must will to be himself and who, in failing to will to be the fullness of himself, inevitably becomes something less than himself. Thus man in history is the fallen creature, the being who again and again fails to accept

[1] Harper, New York, 1959.

the privilege, burden and responsibility of willing to be the fullness of himself. In history man is visibly below the level of his nature and therefore tragically and existentially out of line with his destiny.

It is this condition of being below the level of his nature, and therefore out of line with his destiny, which Christian thought terms original sin. This has been described as the most obviously true of all Christian doctrines—the only Christian doctrine whose truth is evident even upon a simple inspection of the facts. Man in history knows himself as fallen; he knows that he is not what he could be and might have been; he knows, in other words, that there is a tragic chasm between his being and his becoming. This consciousness of being a fallen creature carries with it the implication that as a matter of historical fact he once fell. If the fall were a fall into history rather than a fall in history, there would be no consciousness of being fallen. Then we should say, as apathetic thinkers, who look to theology and philosophy for some kind of alibi in terms of which we can escape the consciousness of being guilty, are always trying to say, that to be what we are in history is to become the only thing which it is possible to be in history, that the sinner is simply conforming to the inherent laws of the context in which he is functioning. We have already rejected this view and we hold that traditional Christian thought was right to insist upon a Fall in history rather than a Fall into history. History is not fallen merely because that is the way all history, any history, has to be, but simply because it is the history of fallen man.

In the course of this discussion we have thus observed two important ontological facts about history. In the first place, history is the habitat of sin. It is not the place in which sin had to happen—there is no such place as that— but it is certainly the only place in which sin could have happened. History, in other words, is the one area of being in which sin is a possibility. In the second place, history is only possible where God has created beings so conscious of themselves, and of the ambivalence of their existence, that it is possible, although never necessary, for their becoming to contradict their being. To use existentialist terminology, existence is no more prior to essence than essence to existence, essence and existence are contemporary, co-real, mutually implicatory principles. We can never escape from the push and pull of either. The concrete reality must always be existence explicit in the essence and essence implicit in the existence. Both the idea of existence apart from essence and the idea of essence apart from existence are useful intellectual abstractions, in terms of which we can think but never live. As between these two there is no question of ontological priority or of logical primacy. But man, the being who makes history, and in turn is partly remade by history, is the being for whom the great civil strife between existence and essence becomes possible. He is the being chronically given to schitzophrenia, and it is from this ontological characteristic of man that history as we know it derives its perennial conflicts and tensions, its characteristic returns to and departures from the way of peace, its happy tragedies and its tragic comedies.

For the history of man is, in the proper sense of the word, a comedy rather than a tragedy. By comedy I do not mean a farce—history is certainly not that—but rather a realistic story containing many unhappy episodes which has, nevertheless, an eschatological resolution, or, as we say in vulgar speech, a happy ending. Of course, each of the many unhappy episodes can be interpreted as a tragedy when seen *sub specie temporis*. To see anything *sub specie temporis* is to see it abstractly, without its ending. History is full of the tragic. Nevertheless, the whole process, viewed *sub specie aeternitatis*, must be interpreted as comedy. Now both the temporal point of view and the eternal point of view are valid, so that the categories both of tragedy and comedy are relevant to the interpretation of the historical drama. Nevertheless, history is the locus of tragedy, while at the same time the process of history as a whole is a comedy, for the eschatological understanding of history, which we find in the Bible, is a religious and theological version or transmutation of the category of the comedy.

> Know that at end,
> Pain was well paid, sweet friend,
> Pain was well paid that brought me to thy side.

The lines are from a sonnet of Francis Thompson, but the judgement is the judgement of the New Testament, or perhaps of a great Christian, eschatological, morality play like Shakespeare's *A Winter's Tale*. In history the tragic episodes are undeniable, but that does not destroy or conceal the comic proportions of the whole drama. This concept of history as comedy brings us to the category of eschatology, and it is to eschatology that we must now turn.

2. Eschatology

The word eschatology means the knowledge of the last thing or things. In the Bible and in early Christianity it is particularly bound up with the belief that the historical order will inevitably culminate in some catastrophic end which will be at the same time a new kind of beginning, for the end of the world is the beginning of the Kingdom of God. Of course, the Christians were not alone even in the ancient world in this belief that the historical order must some day come to an end. Lucretius, for example, holds the same view, although, of course, he expresses it in a very different way. Many, probably most, modern physicists also believe that at last what we know as history will be impossible on this planet, although they would postpone this event to a time very remote from us in the future, and, of course, their 'end of the world' is in no sense the beginning of something conceived of as even better than history. The early Christians seem to have thought that this end of the world was likely to occur very shortly, and it is perhaps because of this logically somewhat extraneous conviction that many modern observers of early Christianity, and even many modern Christians, have fallen into the error of discounting eschatology altogether. The early Christians, such people may say, believed that the end of the world was coming very shortly. Clearly they were wrong, for twenty centuries have ensued since then, and no doubt there are many more to come. This mistake was perhaps the source of all their other errors, and what we need now is a modern Christianity which pays no attention to what we may call the chronic blind spot of the early Christian mentality.

Christianity, according to such critics, must be spiritualized and universalized in manner beyond the ken of the early Christians. It must be seen no longer as primarily a preparation for life in the Kingdom of God, but as primarily a way of purging and improving life on this earth. After all, it was always incidentally a way of purging and improving life on this earth, and so far as we are concerned it is simply a matter of treating as primary what the earliest Christian regarded as secondary. I am convinced that this manner of disregarding something to which the Bible and early Christianity attached such supreme importance is completely mistaken, and I wish to disassociate myself from it entirely. It is not even timely, for, after all, many of our contemporary fears of nuclear war, and our nightmarish imaginings of its worst possible consequences, have for this generation given new currency to the possibility that the historical process might indeed come to an end very shortly, although I doubt whether this is the right way, still less the best way, in which to rediscover the tremendous truth which underlies the eschatological way of looking at history.

The essence of eschatology is really indifferent to the question whether the time that must elapse between now and the end of the world is either a short time or a long time. From the point of view of the New Testament a genuine eschatology is at last possible, because now men already know the last thing. For the last thing is the Christ who will usher in the Kingdom. The last event, whether near to us or far from us, is the reign of the Christ, and in the midst of the Church, the Christian community, that reign has begun already. While still on earth, in time and in history, men in the Church have a genuine participation in the life of the Kingdom of God, so that because Christ is the last thing, the Church is in some sense the last thing also. Thus there is a sense in which we may say that the last thing has happened already. We can know it, of course, as judgement upon what we have become and upon all that we have done in time, but it is also mercy as well as judgement. We can know it as the end of many things that we have loved and valued, but when we discern its character more clearly we see that it is the beginning of our eternal intercourse with all the things that are intrinsically most lovable and valuable. Those who submit to the judgement inherit the promise.

From this point of view we may say that the essential characteristic of Christian existence is this precarious consciousness of existing on the edge of the end of the world. '*Now* is the accepted time: *Now* is the judgement of this world.' From the point of view of the Christian consciousness it is indeed always *now*. The great gospel *now* of judgement and redemption is the vast span of time, as we might say the Christian 'specious present,' in which life is now being lived and the drama of history is now taking place.

Too easily in time we suppose that one moment in time is simply a passage-way leading to another moment in time. We fail to realize that the moments of time are not only successive moments of our own existence but transcended, cumulative moments for the divine consciousness, and in the divine perception of the meaning of history. It was Leopold von Ranke, a historian famous for the purity of his methodology, and for his belief that the aim of the historian was to see each event as it really was, who also tells us that 'every age is immediate to God.' Every moment of history is itself and a thing of value in itself. No moment is a mere passage-way to the next moment. Thus there is in Christianity what we may call a cult of the passing moment, which in some ways affiliates Christianity to the most reckless paganism.

> My candle burns at both ends;
> It will not last the night;
> But, ah, my foes, and, oh, my friends—
> It gives a lovely light.[1]

The intentions of the author of this verse, of course, were neo-pagan rather than Christian, yet by a strange trick of the fancy the stanza defeats the conscious intentions of the poet. How well these lines might be used to describe the earthly career of some great, self-giving saint, like St. Francis of Assisi, utterly devoted to the love of God and to the love of man for God's sake. In *The Family Reunion*,[2] T. S. Eliot has some lines which bring out the same characteristic eschatological quality.

> You bring me news
> Of a door that opens at the end of the corridor,
> Sunlight and singing, when I had felt sure
> That every corridor only led to another.[3]

[1] Edna St. Vincent Millay.   [2] Faber & Faber, London, 1959.
[3] Op. cit., p. 60.

Horizontally, no doubt, it is true that each moment issues out only into another moment, but vertically considered, each moment issues out into eternity. So that for those of us who share this Christian eschatological belief each moment is significant in and for itself. Each moment is crucial; each moment partakes of the character of the last moment. Every moment might conceivably be the world's last moment; indeed, every moment is certainly someone's last moment; any moment might conceivably be my last moment. One linguistic habit we still inherit from this eschatological state of mind is that of describing important events as momentous, although when we consider the indifferent way in which we contrive to squander most of our moments, to say that an event is momentous would not at first sight appear to be saying very much.

In practice, of course, men ignore what we may call the vertical dimension of the moment. They see and interpret this moment only horizontally as related to the next moment and, of course, to the last moment also. Their quest is neither for pie in the sky on the one hand, the pie of the pietist, nor for pie in the present, on the other hand, the pie of the pagan. Their quest is always for pie in the future, the pie of the unrealistic utopian. We seek security in the midst of a life which is inherently insecure, and will no doubt remain so; we seek peace in a world in which there is no peace; we seek social righteousness in a world of fallen men, a public righteousness, politically conceived and imposed, that will not even seek to redeem its beneficiaries and victims; we seek to create a world safe for sinners to sin in, whereas, in fact, no such world is possible. We visualize a golden future in which we shall go on being what we are now, but in which the circumstances and context of our existence will be far better and easier than it is now. We invoke the gods of history and we cry out, 'Save us but do not redeem us.' Most of the time, of course, most of the people delegate this impossible task to their political representatives, punctuating their irresponsibility with occasional seasons of bitter complaint when they ungratefully rebuke the politicians for having so signally failed to do the impossible. 'Jam to-morrow, but never jam to-day.' One is reminded of *Alice Through the Looking-glass* by this strain of crass futility in modern history, by this merely utilitarian conception of the passing moment, by the crass progressivists' belief that the historical condition of man will somehow be improved by the mere lapse of time. Against all this the gospel cries out with its great reiterated NOWS. '*Now* is the accepted time, *now* is the judgement of this world.'[1] For the brief, passing, particularistic NOW of man is the moment at which his narrow vision participates in, is comprehended in, the great eternal all-inclusive *Now* of God. *Now* is or can be the moment in which I am God's and God is mine. *Now* is the moment at which I am under the judgement. *Now* is the moment in which I inherit the promise. Each *now* is pregnant with eternal possibilities.

There is yet another contemporary linguistic habit which recalls this eschatological outlook, the insistent use of the New Testament word *crisis*. In our newspapers, on the TV and the Radio, and again and again in the speeches of politicians, indeed, with almost chronic insistence, we come across the word *crisis*. Our world is passing through a crisis. From the standpoint of the New Testament, however, every *now* is a moment of crisis. The Christian life is lived in the midst of a chronic crisis. *Now* is not the interval between these judgements, 'the gap between two lightnings,'[2] as Francis Thompson said in a fine sonnet, *Now* is the moment of the judgement, *Now* is the flash of the lightning. Of course, to live in the midst of a crisis is uncomfortable, but it is, I would suggest, at

[1] John 12. 31.   [2] Non Pax-Expectatio.

least stimulating and exciting. It is certainly better than that heavy, artificially tranquillized spiritual context and psychic condition, 'peace of mind,' or 'freedom from anxiety,' so overestimated by bogus religionists and uninsightful psychiatrists. We may be grateful that in the twentieth century the horrors of history have set us free from the stupifying hopes and narcotic illusions of *normalcy*, and placed us back in the midst of real history, in the midst of crisis, in a context in which we can bow to the judgement and inherit the promise. For the return to real history is the first step in the return to real and authentic human existence, existence before God who is our Saviour and Judge. We do not know what is going to happen to us in the world. It is even possible that we are all or most of us going to be blown to bits, but at least meanwhile we are not going to be bored. We are back in real history. It is, of course, dangerous. Real history always is, but it is also wildly exciting. The dangers and anxieties innate in historical existence are infinitely worth while.

Of course, this eschatological idea which I have been expounding comes to us primarily from the Bible and from Hebrew thought. Using a technique somewhat reminiscent of Max Müller, many contemporary theologians have pointed out that the Hebrew mind seems to have been much more impressed by the fact of time than by the fact of space, whereas the Greek mind, which is the prototype of all intellectualisms, is more impressed by space than by time. In the same way it would appear that the Greek language was richer in nouns and adjectives which name and describe beings thought of as existing primarily in space, whereas the Hebrew language is more insistent on verbs which observe and record activities carried on in time. No doubt there is a great deal that is true in all this. On the other hand, since both space and time, in fact, exist indissolubly linked in our concrete experience, each way of speaking will have both its strength and its blind spots. From my point of view the weakness of the eschatological language of the Bible, if I may speak in that way, is a by-product of its strength. Because of its preference for temporal language the Bible usually tends to think of the eschaton as something removed from us in time rather than in space. Of course, whether we use spacial or temporal language, we shall be using it analogically rather than literally, composing a sort of philosophic poetry rather than a scientific formula, but I believe that spacial language has something to contribute to our understanding of eschatology. It is never merely that the eschaton is in the future waiting for us just around the corner. Even in the New Testament spacial language is used. The Kingdom of God is not merely in the future; it is also *at hand*, spacially beside us, as well as awaiting us in time. From this point of view man's whole existence in history must be thought of as a continuous existence on the edge or margin of the world.[1]

All human existence, as we have said, takes place on the edge of the end of the world. Man is the missing link, the two-natured creature between the temporal and the eternal, between the creative and the created. He is in the one yet belongs to the other. He strains the limitations of temporal experience almost unbearably and is always pregnant with the possibility of a translation into the eternal. From this point of view we may say that man throughout the whole extent of human time is himself an eschatological being, and it is this which gives our human historical time its primary ontological characteristic. Man's temporality is temporality on the edge of eternity, shot through with the intimations of eternity. That is why I have insisted upon the primacy of the temporal category of the *now*. The past, after all, is a succession of past

[1] See Appendix to Chapter 6, p. 186.

nows. Each moment, in the hour of its concrete actuality, is a *now*. Similarly, the future is a succession of future *nows*. Each future moment at the point at which it reaches concrete actuality will be a *now*. All life is composed of *nows*, and the *now* in which we live and always are is never quite the same thing as an abstract moment plotted on a time chart. Each significant *now* is a cluster of abstract moments transcended and gathered together into a simultaneous unity. Similarly, the great *now* of the eternal, divine existence is, according to the Christian philosophers, all the moments that are or have been or will be gathered into one vast eternal *now*, in the words of Boethius, 'the enjoyment of the fullness of being all at once.'

Man knows eternity as *now*. And he experiences time as a succession of what we may call finite eternal moments, so that even in time his experience has some of the characteristics of eternity. All history is the history of beings who, although in time do not really belong to time with the whole of their being, cannot really lose and find themselves completely in time. History is the temporality of the eternal. In another connection, in the context, that is, of his social philosophy, we can find a similar thought in St. Thomas Aquinas: 'Man does not belong to the political community *secundum se totum* (with the whole of his being), *nec secundum tota sua* (nor with all that is his).'[1] Man, we may say, in a free paraphrase, belongs indeed to society and history, yet never wholly and entirely so, and despite his incapsulation in history and society he possesses attributes that do not properly belong to that picture at all. It is this partial aptitude for history accompanied by other characteristics which make for a rebellion against it, which give history its peculiar flavour as not only a cosmic drama but also a spiritual epic. If history, we may say, is a temporalizing of the eternal, so religion in the

[1] *Summa Theologia*, IIa, 21, 4.

fullest sense of the word is an eternalizing of the temporal. Thus there is between history and religion, which I am understanding now in the sense of biblical revealed religion, a certain innate reciprocity to which I have already drawn attention. Religion is in history and history is for religion. There is no making sense of either without some reference to the other. Religion is historical and history is religious.

3. TIME AND ETERNITY

The notion of time is a complex one, and for our purposes here we may distinguish between three distinct, although not, of course, unrelated, ways of conceiving time. In the first place we may speak of physical time, time as a dimension of physical movement. This is not the same thing as clock time, for nowadays physical motion is measured by far more sensitive and precise instruments than the clocks which we have in everyday use. This kind of time is one we can define by abstraction, using perhaps something like Whitehead's method of extensive abstraction, but it is certainly not the time or duration which we immediately experience. Secondly, we may speak of sociological time, the time in terms of which we interact and co-operate with each other in society. This is the actual clock time of our social experience. Four-fifteen is the time at which I have to call upon Professor So-and-so for an interview. Before the invention of clocks men would say to each other 'I will be ready at dawn,' or 'Meet me outside the Church at sundown.' The clock gives more precision to arrangements of this kind without changing their nature. But even sociological or clock time is not the time of our immediate experience. The time of our immediate experience Bergson called duration. Unlike the more abstract conceptions of time it is not indefinitely divisible into abstract instants. It falls into a finite number of moments each having a duration

173

and character of its own which Bergson called 'the specious present.' In this chapter I have called the specious present by the simple word *now*, the actual time of experience. The time in which man lives is thus very different from abstract physical time. For one thing, abstract physical time is precisely the same for all physical motions whereas duration varies from person to person. If the concert bores me its duration will be interminably prolonged. If it delights me its duration for me will pass like a flash. The more completely enthralled and fascinated we are by any experience, the more it approximates towards an experience of eternity.

The specious present is one meaningful *now*, but we can nevertheless trace within it the pattern of before and after. A single musical phrase, for example, the first four notes of Beethoven's Fifth Symphony, is certainly experienced as one musical phrase in a single specious present, yet the four notes succeed each other in time. If we experience the four notes in their mere successiveness, hearing one at one moment and the next at the next and so on, we should never experience the phrase as a whole at all. Similarly in conversation or in listening to a lecture, the words are, of course, successive, and I hear them successively; nevertheless, I gather one whole sentence into a single specious present and experience its meaning in a single act of the mind. If I simply heard the words in their mere successiveness I should never experience their meaning. Children can sometimes be heard reading in a way that spells out each word in a separate act of comprehension, and the auditor cannot but suspect that they are not really reading at all. My point is that the specious present is in time and concerned with time, but that it yet involves a certain transcendence of mere temporality.

This is indeed an intimation of eternity, for we may say that the eternity of God means that for him the entire course of temporality is gathered into one single specious present. Eternity, as I have said before, is not mere non-time. The notion of the eternity of God no more cuts off God from the world of time than it cuts off the world of time from God. Eternity is time transcended, but neither time nullified nor time ignored. And man himself partakes to a small but significant extent in this kind of eternity. Human experience is again and again an experience of transcendence. For example, the very fact of self-consciousness, the ability to say 'I know me,' the ability to stand over against oneself in criticism and judgement, to be a predicament, an enigma, even a shame, to oneself, involves a certain measure of transcendence, and at the same time, of course, a certain measure of immanence. When I say, 'I know me,' the *I* who knows the *me* in some sense transcends the *me* in knowing him, and yet he is in some sense identical with or at least immanent in the *me* that is known. So that all human experience is honeycombed by significant moments which reflect in miniature the creator's relation to his creation. Man also, in his own small way, is both transcendent and immanent. So that to say that God is transcendent and immanent, far from being a meaningless metaphysical speculation, as some analytical philosophers suppose, is in fact a state-ment which derives its meaning from human experience, or rather from an analogical use of that experience which extends it vastly beyond the arbitrary limitations by which it is hedged about for us, limitations by which for us the experience is always constricted and constrained, but which nevertheless we apprehend as alien to the nature of what we experience. The specious present, as we experience it, is too small and too passing to fulfil its promise. The fullness and perfection of the specious present we must attribute to some more absolute subject than ourselves. We know enough of eternity at least to be able to imagine what it might be like to know it in its totality.

Again we are brought back to the thought of man, created personality, as the link between God and the creation, the eschatological concept of man as the being who stands on the margin of the world, who is indeed in the world and a part of the world, and yet at the same time in the world as the child and representative of God. So that his experience is in part an experience of the world from within the world, and in part an experience *of* the world which represents in miniature an experience of the world from the point of view of the divine transcendence. Ontologically it is this two-natured form of experience which makes history possible and gives the historical drama its own peculiar characteristics. History once more is the presence in time of creatures who do not belong to time with the whole of their being, a being which partakes of the characteristics of both the time which is transcended by eternity and of the eternity which transcends time.

It is this that makes of man a character in the historical drama. From this human existence derives its peculiar poignancy and its extraordinary and exhilarating complexity. If history is the drama which takes place on the margin or circumference, on the outermost edge of the rind of the creation, that which lies beyond history, the next thing to history, so to speak, is God. This accounts for the peculiar consanguinity of history and religion of which I have already spoken. Whenever we have a system of thought for which the concept of the reality of God and the divine purpose is less well developed and articulate than the concept of nature, whenever we have a philosophy which emphasizes and recognizes more easily that which exists beneath man than that which exists above him, there we have a philosophical point of view which cannot do justice to the tensions of history, which cannot understand the dimensions of historical existence. Where religion is lost sight of, man is denatured and his history ceases to be an epic. Man torn between the creator and the creation, in some sense belonging to both and in some sense partaking of the nature of both, is rather in the situation of the hapless, helpless child of divorced parents. He cannot solve his problem by affirming the one and denying the other, nor by cleaving to the one and ignoring the other. Still less can he accept both in their unnatural isolation from each other. Ultimately the only alternative to the redemption of all men is some degree of human and historical schizophrenia.

A philosophical ontology of history, a study of where it is on the scale of being that history takes place, of the metaphysical significance of the fact that it takes place at all, of the basic characteristics of the kind of being for whom and in whom it takes place, thus brings us at last to the same verdict as our study of biblical eschatology. Human existence is poised precariously on the edge of the end of the world. It is useless for man to seek any other habitat than that which is native to his being. Situated anywhere else he would be like a fish out of water. Even to wish for any other habitat is to wish to be no longer man. We can only wait, grateful for the privilege of the fascinating dramatic existence that we have, until in his own good time the God who gave us our nature shall crown it with its destiny.

4. FREEDOM

As we experience it, freedom is essentially the sovereignty of the moment, the causal efficacy of *now*. *Now* is always the accepted time. *Now* is always the crisis of judgement and decision. The reality, the uniqueness of *now* is the basic category in terms of which we are able to think our freedom and affirm it philosophically. Of course, man has always experienced his freedom. The question of freedom as a philosophical issue is not the question whether in fact we experience freedom or not—

that is too obvious even to merit discussion—rather it is the question of whether we are equipped with the philosophical categories which enable us to think it. There are many brands and species of human philosophy which cannot think in terms of freedom, and for them, of course, the question is whether we are to be so governed by a philosophical system as to deny the reality of the experience that we cannot think, or whether the reality of the experience that the system cannot think is not a solid ground for doubting the validity of the system. Something is surely wrong with any philosophical system which is incapable of interpreting the fact of freedom.

Yet generations of dogmatic philosophers have not in practice doubted the validity of their philosophical systems because they were unable to interpret manifest experience. Rather than tackle the laborious task of rethinking their philosophies, they have usually preferred to put the telescope to the blind eye and forget all about the experience, at all events while philosophizing. They could hardly succeed in forgetting it while actually existing.

Determinists who deny the reality of human freedom have in the past relied primarily on some dogmatically asserted concept of causality. According to them we live in the midst of a universal reign of cause and effect, plotted along an abstract time scale which is neither physical time nor sociological time nor existential time, although much closer to physical time than to either of the others, because this time scale, like physical time, does not allow for the reality and sovereignty of *now*. *Now*, I have insisted, is the primary element in a philosophical notion of time, because every moment is *now* at the point of its concrete actuality. But if we have an abstract conception of the moment, which deliberately forgets that every moment is *now* at the point of its concrete actuality, we arrive at an apathetic doctrine of time for which abstract moments are strung along beside each other like peas in a pod, very much like the abstract points in Euclidian space. In this way we arrive at an apathetic doctrine of time to which the existential concept of *now* is irrelevant. The 'nowness' of *now* becomes a kind of accident. The difference between past, present and future is glossed over as merely relative. In their abstract character as mere moments in time they are all identical, with the one exception that, according to this account of the matter, the earlier moments determine the later ones. No moment in any way determines itself, because every moment is determined by its predecessors. On the other hand, each moment, once it has passed the point of its concrete actuality, becomes a determinative moment, because now it begins to contribute to the determination of its successors.

It was always an incredible doctrine. What the moment could not do at the point of its concrete actuality it suddenly begins to do at all subsequent moments, i.e. exercise determinative or causal power. The old determinist writers used to make great play with the notion of what they called chains of cause and effect, but in fact they were thinking in terms of chains of effects, for each moment at the point of its concrete actuality was pure effect. Only after the point was passed did it turn into pure cause. As concrete reality it was pure effect, but when it had ceased to be concrete reality then it became cause. One is reminded of spiritualist doctrines according to which, once the body is destroyed and gone, some kind of peculiar overtone of its physical existence still inhabits the world. So, for this kind of determinism, the moment only begins to operate after it is dead.

Causality conceived in this way is ultimately derived from the idea of fate or the fates in Greek and other mythologies. Indeed, we may say that many of the ideas of causality which survived for so long in scientific thought were mere relics of Greek mythology. For the mythology of the Greeks not only preceded the development of Greek science and philosophy, but also greatly influenced it, so that even now some of our still current scientific concepts are only Greek mythology heavily disguised. For example, any idea of some one primitive *Ur-stoffe*, of which all things are supposed to be composed, is merely a relic of the Greek mythological notion of the chaos out of which all things were made. To say this is to explain why, in its most highly developed forms, the tendency of scientific thought is to rid itself of the concept of causality and to substitute therefore some further complication of its mathematics. Causality is, after all, an occult force. In addition to the plain ascertainable phenomenal or conjectured characteristics of the things we are investigating, we are supposed to add another characteristic, its peculiar degree of causality or causal effectiveness, which is in some sense distinct from all the other things and, as Hume pointed out long ago, is something attributed to things that is never, in fact, experienced or found in things. This occult, supernatural character of causality is perhaps explained for us when we see that it is a survival of mythological notions of inexorable fate.

Primitive or mythological religion seems to deal in two kinds of divine reality. There are the high gods of the light who dwell above men, sometimes in the sky, sometimes in the tops of mountains, and they, from their point of vantage, see down deeply into the hearts of men. But side by side with these 'Sky Gods' we find, in mythological polytheism generally, gods, or more often perhaps the earth goddess, who dwell below us in the bowels of the earth. Their business is done in the darkness. They are concerned with magic and the invisible, inscrutable purposes that determine our fate. Causality in its origins is one of these. An invisible inscrutable power inherent in things by means of which one thing sways and determines another. It is small wonder that the attempt to turn this into a scientific concept is gradually proving a failure.

Nowadays we attempt to substitute a doctrine according to which the mathematics characteristic of a particular structure of events perhaps implies, perhaps merely renders intelligible, the mathematics characteristic of some subsequent structure of events. Whether it actually implies it or merely renders it intelligible—more often, given some principle of indeterminacy, the latter than the former—it is certainly mathematically continuous with it. To attribute to the former state of affairs some occult power or influence called causality becomes unnecessary. Of course, it is then discovered that the mathematical account of the preceding situation which is mathematically continuous with the mathematical account of the succeeding situation, and thus renders it intelligible, might equally well be mathematically continuous with various conjectured configurations alternative to the one which actually occurs. So that out of a whole range of alternative possibilities, which ever one happens would be equally intelligible. The consequence of this is that prediction must be in terms of probability rather than necessity, and the ghost of Greek mythology is exorcised from science at last.

There is, however, an entirely different approach to the problem and nature of causality, one which Hume in his brilliant sceptical analysis of the notion never even noticed. In our personal human existence we are aware of the fact that we do indeed act causally. In the service of our purposes and for the implementation of our choices we intervene again and again decisively in the course of events, so that we can truly say that if we had not purposed as we did and acted as we did, things would not have turned out as, in fact, they have. Whether physical science needs the notion of causality or not, the history and philosophical interpretation of man cannot possibly do without it.

Indeed, we require the notion of causality in order to state any possible doctrine of human freedom. To say that man is free is to say that man, human decision, human choice, human activity and self-mastery, even human apathy and submission to the prevailing currents of the time, is causally operative. Man is a causal agent, and since human decision is made in the *now*, at the crucial moment in which man always finds himself, we may say that this category of the *now* is the category above all others in which it is possible intelligibly to think man's freedom. For the *now* is not merely this particular moment, one in a succession of moments so entirely like each other that we cannot discriminate between them—moments so conceived are mere abstractions, not concrete reality—the *now* is this unique moment, in which I discern the possibility of exercising causal activity not only upon things other than myself but even upon myself. *Now* is not the mere resultant of past moments, *now* is above all the cause of future moments. To interpret this *now* as caused by its predecessors, and in some mysterious way as something that becomes a cause only after it is dead, is to misinterpret and erroneously describe the basic character of *now* as we experience it. The past at least looks determined because it is forever fixed; the future can at least be thought of as determined because, not yet having experienced it, I am free to think of it in any way that I choose, and I have nothing in the light of which to check the accuracy of my conceptions. But *now* I experience as free, for the *now* is the concrete actuality engaged in the very moment of its brief passage in imposing its tiny quota of causal power upon the course of events. Always it is *now* that I am free. And since the whole stream of historical, existential time is composed of a succession of sovereign *nows*, it must clearly be true that I am free all the time, for as we have said every moment at the point of its concrete actuality is a *now*. *Now* is the point at which we immediately experience time.

Thus, from this point of view, causality is no longer something that is done in the darkness, no longer a brooding occult subterranean fate, but rather something that is done in the light. Causality is a property of personality. We can have no possible ground either in science, philosophy or experience for attributing causality to some sub-personal reality, though we may perhaps trace some analogues of freedom even there. Of course, the kind of causality which we experience in our freedom is very frail, finite and limited, hedged about with qualifications and limitations alien to its nature. Absolute freedom and causality, the causality and freedom that we know but unrestricted and unlimited, we attribute absolutely to the Absolute Person, God, and to him alone. Like the eternity of God, the causality and freedom of God is not a meaningless, metaphysical speculation. We attribute to God the absolute person, an unqualified form of that which we discover in the experience of the finite, creaturely person in its qualified form. In God this causality and freedom is utterly true to its nature, hedged about by no restrictions alien to its nature. To God then we attribute pure freedom and pure causality, and in this sense we may agree with Croce's dictum that all history is the history of freedom. But we should mean not that all history is the history of man's gradual attainment and achievement of freedom, rather all history is the history of God's freedom. For all history, as we have already said, is for God one single all-engulfing *now*, and *now* is essentially in its concrete actuality the moment of freedom.

I will make no more than a mere mention of one profound mystical development of this theory, the view that man's finite creaturely freedom is essentially his participation, understood in an almost platonic sense, in the majesty of the divine freedom. God's service according to the collect in the Anglican office for Morning Prayer is perfect freedom, and according to St. John's Gospel the truth which Christ reveals is the truth that makes us free, precisely because it is the truth about the eternal purposes of the divine freedom. It is thus, by realizing that our freedom is ours to make it his, by making human freedom the instrument of divine freedom, that man rises from the creaturely freedom of his *now* into the absolute freedom of that vast divine *now* in which all time and all space is confounded, by which all time and all space is transcended.

'Some sages, however,' says the Saxon King Alfred the Great, in his very free translation of Boethius' *Consolations of Philosophy*, 'say that fate rules both weal and woe of everyman. But I say, as do all Christian men, that it is providence (the Divine purpose) that rules them, not fate.'[1] The point is that we must submit to fate whether we like it or not, whereas men are the servants, indeed, the friends, of providence. In the service of providence men are free; in submission to fate, however resigned and philosophical, they are slaves. Centuries after the first great English king was dead, a Christian poet, G. K. Chesterton, wrote a long ballad about him which elaborated the same basic idea in simple direct terms which comes to us with all the force of a message for the times in which we live. The defeated Alfred sees in a vision the saintly figure of the Mother of Christ and begs her to tell him whether in fact he will succeed in overcoming the Danish invaders of his kingdom. In reply she refuses to provide any kind of comfortable or optimistic prediction:

> The gates of heaven are lightly locked,
> We do not guard our gold,
> Men may uproot where the worlds begin,
> Or read the name of the nameless sin;
> But if he fail or if he win,
> To no good man is told.

[1] Bahn, London, 1864, p. 225.

The men of the East may spell the stars,
And times and triumphs mark,
But the men signed with the Cross of Christ
Go gaily in the dark.

I tell you naught for your comfort,
Yea, naught for your desire,
Save that the sky grows darker yet
And the sea rises higher.

Night shall be thrice night over you,
And heaven an iron coat,
Do you have joy without a cause,
Yea, faith without a hope?[3]

The doctrine of providence may perhaps at times seem inferior to the doctrine of fate precisely because it cannot tell us what is going to happen. On the other hand, the doctrine of providence at least reassures us that we are going to have some effect upon what is going to happen, and at least it reminds us that even though we do not know what is going to happen, we do know what the future course of history, whatever it may be, will be about. We know what the issues are. The privilege of living as a character in an epic can hardly fail to be a costly one; only with a great sum can a man attain this freedom. It is useless to complain about the high costs when the expenditure is in any case inevitable, and the satisfaction to be obtained is literally priceless. There is no evading the sternness of the gospel. The fullness of life is for those who lay it down. The supreme moment of possession is when we give. The symbol of victory and survival is a cross.

[1] *The Ballad of the White Horse.* Methuen, London, 1911. Book I. 'The Vision of the King.'

APPENDIX TO CHAPTER 6

I AM indebted to my colleague, Professor Carmino de Catanzaro, for the following notes about the use of spatial language in an eschatological context in the Old Testament. We may classify such terms under the headings of (*a*) location in space and (*b*) motion in space.

(*a*) We may instance here *qarôb* meaning 'near' or 'close,' often rendered in English translations of the Bible as 'at hand.' This word is frequently used with reference to the eschatological 'day of Yahweh.' For example, in Isaiah 13. 6:

> Wail, for the day of Yahweh is near (*qarôb*)
> as destruction from the Almighty it will come!

or in Ezekiel 30. 3:

> The day is near, (*qarôb*)
> the day of Yahweh is near;
> it will be a day of clouds,
> a time of doom for the nations.

Similarly, in Zephaniah 1. 14:

> The great day of Yahweh is near (*qarôb*)
> near (*qarôb*) and hastening fast.

There are other references to the same effect in Joel 1. 15; 4. 14; and Obadiah 15.

The use of the term in other eschatological connections is analogous. Thus the statement is put into the mouth of Balaam in Numbers 24. 17:

> I see him, but not now
> I behold him, but not nigh (*qarôb*)

referring either to the Israel of the future or the king which is to rise in Israel, in a setting that may well be intended as eschatological in a rudimentary sense. More specifically 'eschatological' would be a reference such as Isaiah 12. 22, 'Its time is close at hand (*qarôb*).'

(*b*) References to motion are also frequent, often in close connection with location in space. Here the verbs *bô*, 'to come,' and *māhēr*, 'to hasten,' are common. Thus in Isaiah 56. 1, we have an expression of both categories (*a*) and (*b*): 'soon (*qerôbah*) my salvation will come (*la bô*),' and similarly in Joel 2. 1:

> The day of Yahweh is coming (*bá*, literally 'has come'),
>   it is near (*qarôb*)

Zephaniah, in 1. 14, has described the day of Yahweh as 'near (*qarôb*) and hastening (*māhēr*) exceedingly.' We do not, however, find in this connection the verbal root *qarâb*, 'draw near,' corresponding to the adjective *qarôb*, in any of its forms, active or causative. In a few cases the verbal form stands alone, without the adjective of location in its immediate context—as in Isaiah 13. 9:

> Behold, the day of Yahweh comes (*bá* literally 'has come')
>   cruel, with wrath and fierce anger.

or in Malachi 4. 5 (cf. *Heb.* 3. 23)—'Behold, I will send you Elijah the prophet before the great and terrible day of Yahweh comes (*bô*).'

It would appear that the Bible does not discriminate too clearly between spatial and temporal categories, and often uses the one as a metaphor for the other. Obviously in many places the spatial is a metaphor for the temporal. That is perhaps familiar and generally accepted. What we have suggested is that at least sometimes the temporal may be used as a metaphor for the spatial. Of course, more philosophically understood, the relationship between time and eternity, between the process of preparation and the glory of consummation, between the City of Man and the City of God, or between salvation history and salvation itself, is neither temporal nor spatial, but the imagery in terms of which we assert it can and should be drawn from both experience of space and experience of time. To use either type of imagery to the exclusion of the other can only give us a very one-sided view of the reality to which all our images refer. In fact, however, we have tended to use temporal images, or a temporal interpretation of biblical images, to a degree which in effect excludes spatial images, and in that way we have somewhat narrowed and misinterpreted the fullness of the biblical teaching.

CHAPTER 7

TRANSCENDENCE *OF* AND *IN* HISTORY

HISTORY, we have agreed, is essentially time transcended: but there are different degrees and modes of transcendence, so that we must now be more explicit.

In the first place time is transcended absolutely by God, who is not subject to the limitations inherent in temporal, historical existence. In saying this we have been careful to emphasize that God's eternity is more than a mere non-time, so that his transcendence of time in no way belittles time or robs it of significance. Time transcended, we have said, is not time nullified, nor does God's transcendence of time imply that for him time goes unmarked and unknown. God knows all that he transcends in the very act of transcending it, for, indeed, transcendence is one of the characteristic consequences of conscious knowledge.

In the second place we have said that man also, in his own way and to his own finite degree, transcends history in knowing it, just as he transcends himself in knowing himself. Man, we have pointed out, knows himself as in history and for history, but he also knows himself as a being in some degree independent of history, as one who exists at the same time in God and for God, that is, he knows himself as an individual, as a whole as well as a mere part of a whole. We have seen that it is characteristic of this situation that for man there is always possible a schism in his being, threatening to sunder and separate that in him which is in and for history from that in him which is in and for God.

It is this schism in the soul, so characteristic of life in a fallen world, that gives to the historical drama as we know it its perennial characteristics. That is why, for example, in the Augustinian doctrine, history is and must be a tale of two cities, a story of persistent strife punctuated with uneasy epochs of comparative peace. Part at least of the meaning of the term redemption is the final resolution of this tension, man's attainment at long last of a becoming which befits his being, the emergence of a new mode of history which will truly express history's relation to the eternal purpose of God and man's relation to the eternal purpose of his own being. We may speak of this emergence as the end of history and the beginning of the Kingdom of God, using the language of the Bible, or we may use the language of Karl Marx and speak of the beginning of true history, dismissing all that has gone before as no more than a frustrating caricature of history. Of course, I should prefer to use biblical language, but it must be said that the doctrines are basically the same whatever language we use.

In addition we may speak of a transcendence of history by historical episodes themselves wherever and whenever they so capture the consciousness and imagination of succeeding generations as to inspire, encourage or afright people across great gaps of time. There are some historical episodes at least which refuse to die or pass away, which can still rouse passions or inspire faith long after their day is done. We may say that in their own way episodes such as these transcend history. One very characteristic form of this kind of transcendence is the persistent relevance— we might almost call it the eternal youthfulness—of great artists and poets whose work provides deep delight for generation after generation. 'Thou wast not for an age, but for all time.'

Again, there are certain great conflicts which still retain the power to divide men centuries after they are over. Few of us feel tempted to fight the Wars of the Roses over again, but the Civil War of the seventeenth century between the English King and Parliament to this day retains the power to set Englishmen debating against each other, and the Civil War between North and South in America has something of the same character. These wars were concerned with controversies between human beings which still persist, and, indeed, the very memory of the wars has played no inconsiderable part in keeping such differences alive. It is not simply that these facts are known. There are many known historical facts which can be cognized quite apathetically, without raising any partisan impulses in the knower, but of certain events this is not true. Of their own momentum they seem to demand sympathy and decision. We cannot merely narrate them and locate them accurately in the past; we feel even at this late date impelled to declare where we ourselves stand with regard to them. We may say of such events that in their own measure, and within the limits characteristic of this mode of transcendence, they do indeed transcend history, that they remain relevant to our consciousness and exercise causal and persuasive influence long after history has seemingly brought them to a conclusion.

Of transcendent events of this kind it is obviously true that for all Christians, and for many non-Christians whose non-Christianity is a matter of conscious decision, incomparably the most important of the events having this character are those to which the gospels testify. The complex Christ-event is certainly, from one point of view, a succession of particular events now long ago concluded, but for Christianity they are in a sense universal events, events which have a relevance and significance wherever men are men, so that the mere recollection and narration of them has at the same time perennial metaphysical significance and undiminished causal power. The Christ-event certainly took place in history, yet in a very real sense we can see it as an event which transcends all history and exercises upon the course of all history a certain sovereign pressure.

We have thus distinguished three modes of transcendence, God's transcendence of all time and history, man's finite transcendence of his own time and history, and the actuality of certain transcendental historical episodes of which the Christ-event is incomparably the most important. Before, however, embarking upon any more extensive discussion of these distinct modes of transcendence it might be well to examine more carefully the meaning of the word transcendence itself, although that perhaps will be one way of making clear what we mean by transcendence in the absolute sense of God's transcendence of his creation.

Transcendence is not mere otherness. That is why in Christian theology God is declared to be not only transcendent of the creation but also immanent within the creation. Nor is this a bleak paradox which cannot be resolved. We often encounter in philosophy pairs of ideas so subtly interrelated that it can almost never be correct to refer to the one without referring to the other, so that it must always be misleading and invalid to affirm the one while denying the other, and altogether impossible to interpret reality in terms of the one while ignoring the other. In common speech we have concepts like north and south or left hand and right hand. In each case there is a clear distinction but also mutual implication. It would be impossible to conceive the world as a pure north without any trace of south, or as altogether to the left with none of it anywhere on the right. In philosophy we encounter similar distinctions, like that between subject and object, and here we find mistakes being made of which common speech would never be guilty. There are thinkers, for example, who attempt to give an account of the world in exclusively objective terms, and others, equally perverse, who commit the opposite error of holding that all truth must be subjectively conceived and defined. The same thing is true of transcendence and immanence. Neither can be conceived or properly defined without reference to the other. Transcendence without immanence is mere otherness, not real transcendence at all. Immanence without transcendence is mere identity, not real immanence at all. Real transcendence is always the transcendence of the immanent, just as real immanence is always the immanence of the transcendent.

In the twentieth century we have had a whole generation of theologians who made much too much of the immanence of God, and supposed that they could do so by ignoring or minimizing the transcendence of God. The inevitable result was the kind of reaction which we find in Karl Barth, who sometimes writes as though he supposes that the best way of affirming the transcendence is to ignore or minimize the immanence. Of course, Karl Barth has a context in intellectual history. In particular he comes after a long period of the so-called liberal theology, which was accustomed to insist so strongly on the metaphysical kinship of divine and human personality that for it the perfection of human personality is divinity, so that it was prepared to speak of Christ as divine simply because he was the perfect man. From this point of view to say that Christ is truly man, human nature and personality in the ultimate perfection of its development, is the same thing as to say that Christ is truly divine. To be perfect man or, better perhaps, to be man perfectly is to be God.

Now, of course, Christian orthodoxy has always held that there is indeed a kinship between human and divine personality, so that analogies drawn from the one may rightly be employed, indeed, must necessarily be employed, in speaking of the other. Nevertheless, Christian orthodoxy has always held that the distinction between uncreated divine personality and created human personality remains absolute. It must stop short at analogy and never presume to claim identity. Barth, however, in the full flood of righteous reaction roundly declared that God is the *wholly* other, with the inevitable consequence that he felt compelled to deny the validity of even that analogy between divine and human personality on which traditional orthodoxy had so strongly insisted. We can understand and sympathize with the heat and extent of his reaction, but it is, nevertheless, one which orthodox Christian thought cannot approve. If Christianity cannot be turned into a purely liberal doctrine on the one hand, it is not totally illiberal on the other. However much, in the course of sinful history, the image of God in man may have been defaced, man remains the being made in the image of God, so that the validity of analogy can never be excluded. We may contrast with Barth's declaration that God is wholly other a characteristically more moderate and judicious phrase of the English theologian, W. R. Matthews, 'God is the beyond who is akin.'[1] This at least keeps both transcendence and immanence in view. The beyond who is akin is perhaps only another way of describing the transcendent who is immanent and the immanent who is transcendent. Transcendence, then, is more than mere otherness; immanence is less than mere identity. There is no kind of contradiction or tension between these two notions, rather each implies and necessitates the other.

We have already noted that in its own much smaller way man's transcendence of history possesses the same characteristics. The man who transcends history is also the man who is in history, indeed, he only transcends history by knowing himself to be in history, by experiencing the arbitrary limitations of historical existence. To know oneself as in history is at least to experience the possibility of being oneself in some different environment.

[1] *God in Christian Thought and Experience.* Nesbitt, London, 1930, p. 10.

He who knows himself as being in history knows himself as a being who could conceivably be out of history, experiences historical existence not only as opportunity but also as frustration, experiences history as something which at the same time confers a freedom to be and yet takes it away. Self-conscious existence in history finds itself confronted by a reality characteristically ambivalent. To be in history is always to be beckoned in two directions at the same time.

History, as we have already seen, has two dimensions, a horizontal dimension in which one moment intervenes as a mere link between the next moment and the last, and a vertical dimension in which each moment is for God, in which each moment insists on being triumphantly itself rather than the mere conclusion of the last moment or the mere prelude to the next. It is this ambivalence or double character of history which makes historical existence the grievous burden of responsibility, the perplexing predicament, which it so frequently is. If only we were all animals it would be so much simpler, in a real sense freer, more spontaneously natural and joyous. Here we find the source of the perennial attractions of various brands of neo-paganism and the persistence of forlorn and solitary demands for some kind of return to nature, vegetarianism, nudism, cults of the noble savage, and so on. Even in Toynbee's writing we come across an idealized picture of the pigmies of central Africa, which has something of the same effect.

Behind all this lies some kind of desire either to return to the womb or even to go back on evolution and social development, to go back on the emergence of man as man. Of course, it is not surprising if we find that being fallen man, being human in a fallen world, is again and again tragic and unpleasant, and it always involves bearing a burden of 'dreadful freedom' through life. Yet to wish for any great reversion of the evolutionary process is to desire the impossible. In scripture there is no return to the Garden of Eden. The Bible does not end with a procession back to the Garden led by Christ carrying his cross and composed of a great company of redeemed saints casting their garments joyfully aside as they approach the Garden gates. The Bible certainly begins in a garden, but it ends in a city, the City of God.

Civilization, from the biblical standpoint, is something which God wills, a burden which rebellious man cannot escape, and a joy which obedient, redeemed men shall yet experience. In a fallen world, of course, we know only civilization in its suicidal, perverted mood, civilization always threatening to poison itself with war and corruption, and sometimes at least actually fulfilling its threats. Yet civilization, even as we know it, is shot through with analogies to the Kingdom of God, which make it a rewarding as well as an intimidating process. Civilization is God's will and its values, however perverted and misapprehended, remain in the last resort God's values.

Thus man experiences his transcendence as a dreadful and perplexing predicament. He experiences himself in history, a fallen being in a fallen history, and yet in transcending this situation he knows and declares himself to exist both for God and for eternity. The world in which he is immanent is engaged in fighting a rebellious war against the world which he claims and inhabits in virtue of his transcendence. Transcendent man is identical with his immanent self, and yet at the same time he is constrained to repudiate his immanent self. He affirms himself at one moment and then judges himself at the next. 'I am not,' he says, 'what I am.' Despite the insistence of the neo-orthodox theologians, it is man not God who is the paradoxical being; man, not God, who is irrational, because the universe of his own soul, in its chronic schismatic condition, is indeed an irrational state of affairs. Sin is the true absurd. Looking within himself and finding his own confusion irrational, the too subjective thinker is prone to suppose that his irrational condition is the condition of all things, but that does not necessarily follow. It is only his rationality which enables the contemporary existentialist to perceive his absurdity. Nothing is absurd except from a rational point of view. It may well be that there is no coherent rationale of fallen existence, but there will certainly be a coherent rationale of redeemed existence, for redeemed existence will be existence in its wholeness, existence altogether for God. The Christian thinker may very well object to the merely shallow rationalist, who declares that everything is quite rational now as things are in this world, but he must do so in a way which does not betray him into dogmatic irrationalism. It is certainly part of his faith that all things will be absolutely rational in the Kingdom of God, for God himself is the architect and fount of all reason. Here and now we are rational beings caught in an irrational state of affairs, we are eternal beings involved in a temporal state of affairs, we are beings who exist for God caught in a web of circumstances so tangled that we may easily suppose that we are beings who exist for ourselves, or even beings who exist pointlessly, *for* nothing at all. We are the children of light engulfed in the darkness, the heirs of God's kingdom frustrated and perplexed because we cannot find abiding satisfaction and fulfilment among the kingdoms of men.

But perhaps the most vivid manifestation of man's transcendence of that particular patch of historical development by which he is surrounded, and in which he finds himself inextricably involved, is to be found in those moments and moods in which men are impelled by experience to constitute themselves the critics and judges of the historical process. If the Hebrew prophets are one outstanding example of this experience, the revolutionary politics of the left-wing tradition provides us with another.

At such times it is as though men find within themselves the criteria in the light of which a particular phase of human history and of the development of social institutions must be judged. Thus the prophetic outburst in the Old Testament judges the performance of Hebrew history and the structure of Hebrew institutions from the standpoint of the purpose and will of God, made manifest in the deliverance of the people under Moses and in the creation of the new Chosen Nation once it had occupied and made its own the promised land.

Centuries later a new tradition of always radical and sometimes revolutionary politics is born when men begin to contrast the actualities of history around them with some sense of a natural law which prescribes and describes what social and personal life would be like if at long last they were to accommodate and express the true underlying human nature, which all history from the beginnings until now has suppressed and concealed.

Inevitably where this tradition was in revolt not only against society as it is but also against Christianity, the result was a kind of secularized prophecy, a doctrine of a fall with no real sense or expectation of redemption. If in this secularized condition the revolutionary tradition in politics had any sense of redemption at all, man was to redeem himself by violent action, bringing about revolutionary change in the midst of history. From this point of view the redemption, the coming of the new ideal social order, always lies in the future for the politics of the revolutionary tradition, which was thus more akin to Judaism, for which the Messiah has yet to come, than to Christianity, for which the Messiah has come already. Nevertheless, the politics of the revolutionary tradition were, so far as the pure idea at least is concerned, consistent with Christianity and biblical religion, and the fact that it so often parted company with them is a regrettable historical accident rather than an inexorable intellectual necessity. Certainly it embraced a genuine doctrine of the Fall which had some connection with the narrative in the opening chapters of Genesis. 'Man is born free, but is everywhere in chains.'[1] The coming of civilization is the advent of slavery.

It is perhaps not surprising that when freedom was so conceived it often turned out to be the freedom of the savage. When the revolutionary tradition insisted on parting company with Christianity, as it so often did, it gravely injured and distorted itself. It lacked moderation and judicious common sense, and it lacked any reverence for the real achievement of civilization, which is none the less real despite civilizations' many and admitted defects. The resentment and rejection of civilization's achievement to date was too extreme and undiscriminating. It turned easily into a hatred of man's achievement to date and thus into a hatred of man himself. How often it is true that the politics of drastic social reconstruction, which surely needs above all the energies of love, is in fact based upon chronic psychological dissidence, destructiveness and hate. The political ideals often seem broad and generous enough, but always they tend to be accompanied by an impatience with actual living men, and not seldom by a cruel and unsympathetic treatment of many men who seem to stand in the way of these imposing reconstructions. Almost every great revolution is a strange compound of generous words, noble aspirations and detestible actions.

Yet this conviction that each man carries within himself the criteria in the light of which history and society must be judged, and judged absolutely, does involve a genuine sense of man's mysterious transcendence of that historical process in which from any other point of view he would seem to be entirely immersed. Such a state of mind altogether contradicts any kind of historical relativism, according to which man makes no absolute judgement but

[1] Rousseau. *The Social Contract*. Chapter 1.

simply the judgements which reflect the culture and condition of his society. From this non-relativistic point of view man's goal is not merely that of being well adjusted to his society and fitting easily into its structure. On the contrary, man is in a real sense the judge and lord of his society. It must be fitted to him rather than he to it, and in passing judgement upon it he genuinely transcends it. Obviously the Christian can hardly avoid being critical of the revolutionary tradition. It is a crude secularization of his own tradition, to which he can feel intellectually superior; an ethical failure to perceive its deeper sanctions, to which he can feel morally superior; an aesthetic blindness to its spiritual beauties, to which he can feel humanly superior. Nevertheless, the revolutionary tradition is indeed a secularization of his own tradition, and the Christian, however much he may dislike the crude garments in which it clothes itself, is failing in genuine theological discernment if he does not see that even in this bastardized form the revolutionary tradition is of one substance with his own, that it implies the same transcendence of history which his own tradition implies. It implies it, of course, much less intelligently, but it does nevertheless imply it.

We may go further and even say that the Christian should acknowledge that the isolation of the revolutionary tradition from Christianity is at least in part, although certainly not altogether, the fault of past Christian teachers and leaders who, having in obedience to the gospel communicated to modern men the germ of the revolutionary tradition (i.e. the doctrine of man's transcendence of history), failed to add to it any sense of positive and immediate relevance, failed to express it as the ground of any demand for historical action. Of course, we can understand this failure sympathetically. The past triumphs of long dead Christian heroes had brought about a situation in which established western society at least invoked the gospel in principle, with the result that, as it seemed to many Christians, Christendom had already been established. On this assumption Christendom had to be defended in a conservative mood, but nothing more remained to be done so far as creating it was concerned. In their generous desire to acknowledge that the past had accomplished much they forgot that even more yet remained to be done. We can understand and forgive, but, unless we are as blind as our forefathers were, we can hardly agree.

At least, however, Christianity and the revolutionary tradition in modern politics are agreed on certain propositions. (1) There is a tragic disparity between the actual performances of man in history on the one hand and human nature and needs on the other. The kind of society that our history creates neither fully expresses human nature nor completely satisfies human needs. The Christian would say that this must always be so in one way or another, and that man must continually labour on earth to make historical performance more expressive of human nature and more sensitive to human needs, without ever being so presumptuous as to expect total success. Man is in history, but history is for man. History never is and never can be so completely successful, so perfect morally and aesthetically, as to justify a merely conservative attitude towards its achievements. (2) Man is in history, yet as moral and historical agent man transcends history. He is the being who carries within himself the seeds of judgement. In the last resort man makes history and not history man. Man, under God, is history's proper lord. The Christian, of course, would attach the utmost importance to the qualification 'under God,' because unless we make and deeply feel this qualification we shall commit the error of supposing that history's proper Lord is an arbitrary, tyrannical, lordless lord, and in consequence grossly exaggerate the freedom and potentiality of man's mastery over history. The historical time allotted to his care is something for which he is answerable; in the revolutionary tradition, of course, answerable to other men, particularly to the unborn generations; in the Christian tradition, answerable to God, who will certainly ask of each one of us on Judgement Day, 'What did you do with the time I entrusted to you?'

Thus we find in our culture two kindred traditions, however estranged, which both agree that there is a sense in which man transcends history, that man is a responsible being answerable not merely to those round about him but answerable also to the ages, and therefore, however dimly this may sometimes be perceived, to the eternal God of the ages, the ancient of days who remains perennially young, the eternally creative creator.

Now let us turn to the third mode of transcendence, the concurrence of events in history which somehow transcend all historical change, events which haunt all subsequent history, remaining, so to speak, contemporary in every age. We have already remarked that the most obvious examples of this process are aesthetic, on the way in which works of human genius in the arts contrive to reaffirm and re-establish their values in generations and cultures increasingly remote from their own. But by far the most impressive and vivid instance of this process is the permanent and universal relevance of the Christian experience of Christ and, since this is the instance most germane to our present discussion, it is upon this most absolute and revealing example of the transcendence of history by history that we shall concentrate in our present discussion.

Croce, writing from within the idealist tradition of philosophy deriving ultimately from Hegel, developed the view that all history is contemporary. When we inquire as to precisely what he meant by this strange dictum we experience a certain disappointment. The substance of his doctrine is less exciting than its formulation. The mere assertion 'all history is contemporary' cannot but remind the Christian thinker of the great cry of Jesus in the Fourth Gospel, 'Before Abraham was, *I am*,'[1] and of the sense in which, for the Christian doctrine of the communion of the saints, all the redeemed are ultimately contemporary in the Kingdom of God.

But Croce appears to have in mind rather less than this. The subject-matter of history is not for Croce the past as such, still less the past as it actually was. The subject-matter of history is not the past but that portion of the past of which we possess surviving evidences. History thus results from the contemporary activity of critically sifting surviving evidences. Living historical thought is always contemporary thought, an operation of the living mind which, by experiencing and expressing its own reactions to such evidences of the past as are subjected to its scrutiny, more profoundly experiences itself. To quote Collingwood, who in this matter was close to Croce, 'History is thus the self-knowledge of the living mind. . . . History . . . lives only in the mind of the historian. . . .'[2]

The question is not whether all this is true or not. The truth of the facts sited by the argument is beyond question. The real issue is a different one: Do these facts justify the dictum, 'All history is contemporary'? It would seem to me that they fail to do so. Of course, all present historical thinking is contemporary thinking. But present historical thinking is not even the only kind of historical thinking with which we are acquainted. Among the many evidences which come to us from the past are those which acquaint us with the thinking of dead historians, for example Heroditus and Thucydides. No doubt their thought was contemporary when they thought it, but it can hardly be contemporary for us in the same sense when we merely appreciate, interpret and report it.

[1] John 8. 58.
[2] *The Idea of History.* Oxford University Press, London, 1946, p. 202.

In any case, even though all historical thinking is contemporary, it is essentially contemporary thinking about the past. We find ourselves in the presence of the hoary fallacy of philosophical idealism in a new form. Older idealists had argued that because everything known is something experienced, therefore nothing is known but experience. The doctrine that, since everything we know is something which is known now, it therefore follows that everything we know is contemporary, is a similar example of the same error. The datum of the thought, it is contended, must possess the same characteristics as the thought which thinks it. In the long run all idealism reduces to some variant of the statement that thought can only think itself. But this is surely to mistake and underestimate the characteristics and potentiality of thought, which is always a grasping of the essence of that which is and remains foreign to itself. That is why thought always transcends what it thinks about. But in order to maintain this doctrine of the transcendental character of thought, we must distinguish between the act of thought and its theme. Thought can only be transcendent if it genuinely embraces and includes within itself some element other than itself, which is both reaffirmed and transcended in the very act of thinking it. The essence of thought in other words is to be found in its comprehension of, and intellectual sovereignty over, what we may call non-thought. Thus although all history is contemporary in the immediate moment of historical activity, it also remains true that the aim of historical thought is to grasp something which is not contemporary, i.e. the past.

Nor is our notion of the past simply a speculative metaphysical construction. We all carry within us a sense of our own past, which enables us by analogy to arrive at a wider and more comprehensive notion of mankind's past. It is not difficult to locate events in mankind's past since we already locate an increasing number of events in our own past. Of course, the act of memory by which we may recall our own past is a contemporary act, but what is recalled remains nevertheless a past event. For a being equipped with memory there is inevitably a category of the past. When we are dealing intellectually with our own past we can even, although not always, distinguish between the way in which we look at the event now, when we have acquired the wisdom that comes after the event, with the way in which the event impressed us then. So that this also is a distinction which we can project upon mankind's past. The distinction between how it felt *then* and how it looks *now* is vital for living historical thought. We must know how it felt *then* in order to describe and sympathetically appreciate the past event. We must know how it looks *now* in order to record our contemporary judgement upon it. Croce's historical idealism seems to confuse the question—'How it felt then?' with the question—'How it looks now?' By implication the question, 'How it looks now?' would seem to be the only question that man can ask with any hope of an answer from his own point of view, but this would seem a gross failure to do justice to the great triumphs of the best historical thinking.

Using language already familiar to us in this book, we may say that Croce's theory systematically ignores the ambiguity of the term *history*. For him history is synonymous with our history A, that portion of history which is known to the historian. Because it is known to the historian in the present or, as Croce would prefer to say, because it is thought by the historian in the present, therefore for him all history, interpreted as history A, is contemporary. In the sense of our history B, however, history consists of elements known to and thought by the historian in the present and other elements unknown to and unthought by the historian, yet in history B the two exist side by side in unbroken unity. Thus we grant that there is some sort of case for saying that history A exists in the present, but we must hasten to add that there is no ground whatsoever for the assertion that history B exists in the present. If, therefore, we take the view that history B is the subject-matter of history A, it would appear that we cannot possibly agree that all history is contemporary.

Yet if the dictum 'all history is contemporary" appears on examination to be too sweeping, it does seem to carry with it certain exciting intellectual possibilities. All historical events are, indeed, in some sense in the past, some irrevocably because they have left no evidences behind them. But some historical events at least seem to possess the characteristic of being alive in the present as well as in the past. There is a real sense in which Beethoven's symphonies, although they belong to the cultural history of the early nineteenth century, are nevertheless still very much alive and contemporary for the enthralled audience at the concert. Masterpieces of art and thought sometimes seem to have more life now than they had in the comparatively unimpressed world which saw their birth. In the eighteenth century few people took much notice of the Italian philosopher, Vico, yet now it is quite possible and plausible to say that he was incomparably the greatest thinker of his epoch. He is more alive now than he was in the eighteenth century. Yet these instances are the exception rather than the rule. Most eighteenth-century events are now wholly forgotten, and the number of eighteenth-century events which make this kind of contemporary impression, although unusually large because it was a peculiarly gifted century, is nevertheless finite. Thus many past events are in a real sense contemporary events, although the great majority of them remain merely past.

In the Christian consciousness the Christ-event is the supreme instance of a past event which is also contemporary. That is why the kind of history which merely uses the category of the past, which simply asks what it was, how it felt, how it happened then, while to a great extent ignoring the question of what it means now, has been so singularly unsuccessful in its attempt to grapple with the Christ-event. The nineteenth-century attempt to depict a pure *Jesus of history*, related merely to his own age, systematically ignoring the later experience of the Christian Church, the so-called *Christ of faith*, failed to perceive that in the deepest sense the *Jesus of history* is the *Christ of faith*, that the *Christ of faith* is a wider concept which comprehends and includes the *Jesus of history*, a wider concept because based upon and interpreting a much broader strand of human experience. Perhaps St. Paul was anticipating the modern rejection by the Church of the limitations of the *Jesus of history* school of research when he cried out, 'Henceforth know I Christ after the flesh no more.'[1] The Christian experience of Christ is always primarily the experience of the risen and exalted Christ, living in and for the Christocentric piety of the Christian Church.

Of course, this does not mean that the witness of the New Testament can be ignored; on the contrary, it means that it must be richly prized and carefully treasured; but it does mean that the Church has another access to the mind of Christ beside the New Testament, although never without or apart from it. The phrase *the Jesus of history* is ambiguous. It could mean the Jesus who belongs to history—and that Jesus belongs to history because by his own act he placed himself within history must in some sense be granted; although the Christian would hasten to add that in an even profounder sense all history belongs to Jesus. It could mean Jesus as reconstructed by historical art and research. In this case the *Jesus of history* means little more than the Jesus of the historians. Again, since the Christ-event really occurred in history we must grant that it is possible for the historians to get at it, at least to

[1] 2 Cor. 5. 16.

some extent, by using their own proper arts. Nevertheless, as we have already seen, it cannot be held that all historical events are equally within the historians' reach and grasp, and there must unquestionably have been many events in the life of Jesus which belong to our historical darkness or our historical twilight, although many of them, it is true, 'were not done in a corner' and are to be found in the clear historical daylight in which the historians' writ rightly runs. We cannot possibly say, however, that the historian is the only or even the supreme authority where questions about Jesus are concerned.

Again, the phrase *the Jesus of history* may simply mean that the ultimate Christian appeal is, indeed, to history, whether it is possible for the historian to know it or not. The equally hackneyed dictum, 'Christianity is the historical religion,' certainly does not mean that Christianity is the historians' religion. Rather it means that the Christian's biblical faith is such that it always tends to affirm that what it knows is based upon some kind of historical revelation or disclosure, is rooted in events which really happened in real history, whether it is possible for the historian to perceive them or not. Sometimes both the historian and the Christian will be able to see the event equally clearly—as in the case of the Crucifixion—and in this case they may differ about the event's meaning and revelational character but agree about the actuality. Sometimes, however, the event will be one which occurred in the twilight, like the Resurrection or the so-called Virgin Birth. In this case the historian may hesitate or even reject, but the Christian will nevertheless affirm, simply because to root itself in the event is the chronic Christian habit.

That which differentiates biblical and Christian faith from faith in general, from the kind of faith and foresight, for example, which we find in Greek mystery religions, which has much in common with Bultmann and some contemporary theologians but nothing in common with the Bible and classical Christianity, is this persistent locating of revelation in history. The real difficulty about the trite distinction between the *Jesus of history* and the *Christ of faith* is the failure to see that it is of the essence of the faith which affirms the *Christ of faith* to be indeed the *Christ of faith* to declare that the *Christ of faith* is the *Jesus of history*. No doubt there was something about the *Jesus of history* which compelled his most intimate followers to see and interpret him as the *Christ of faith*, but much more certainly there is something about the *Christ of faith* which compels Christians to identify him with the *Jesus of history*, and this is because Christian and biblical faith is essentially historical faith, a uniquely biblical kind of faith which is willing, when necessary, to make even historical affirmations on the ground of faith alone. We must not interpret the *Jesus of history* as a kind of constraint on faith, rather we must see the characteristically Christian historical affirmations as themselves the verdicts of a faith which insistently thrusts itself into history.

All this may perhaps give us some insight into the Christian impatience with those more pedantic historians who merely want to tell us who or what Jesus *was*. For the Christian the Christ *is*. In the Church he is known as well as recollected, genuinely contemporary rather than a figure from the remote past who has left a fascinating series of records which enable us to reconstruct his historical face. It is true that part of Christian life has always been a solemn liturgical recollection or anamnesis of the *Jesus of history*, but this is much more than the mere remembering of one who is dead and gone, indeed, to remember in the literal sense, in the way in which Jesus is re-membered in the Eucharist, is to re-knit into, re-include within, the body of living, contemporary experience the reality of Christ. Similarly to recollect God in the act of prayer is not simply to recall past episodes in which God revealed himself, but to become immediately aware of the living, contemporary, urgent reality of the Lord of the universe. From this point of view Christ is, indeed, always an element in immediate contemporary experience, and we must examine more carefully the actual ways and forms in which this re-membering or recollection takes place. What is it in Christian experience that provides the context in which it is possible for the apparently remote Christ to reaffirm his contemporary reality and presence for the Christian consciousness?

We have then to consider this question: How, in fact, does Christ, the ascended Lord and head of the Church, in the experience of Christians, communicate to one generation after another this deep sense and conviction of abiding presence and power. Of course, this book is written from the standpoint of Christian faith and we may well say that no historical strategem could succeed in communicating this particular conviction were it not, in fact, true. Christ is continually present in and through and to his Church, so that the technique by means of which this sense of his presence is communicated possesses the tremendous advantage of endeavouring to communicate something which is real and communicable. Nevertheless, however much we may approve of that which is communicated, we can still ask the question: 'Precisely how is this particular communication made?' A proposition of Euclid is just as valid in French as it is in Russian. It is delivered in French when a French school teacher addresses French pupils and in Russian when a Russian school teacher addresses Russian pupils. Thus we must always distinguish between the mode and manner of the communication and the substance itself of that which is communicated. Even the most efficient modes of communication are rendered weak and ineffective when they devote themselves to communicating some invalid and baseless message. What we are considering here are the ways in which the great truths of the transcendence and omnipresence of Christ is given to and preserved in the conscious minds of generations of Christian.

I shall speak here of three vehicles by means of which the Christ gives himself to the ages: (1) Evangelical preaching, arousing its concomitant, faith; (2) Liturgy, fostering its inevitable consequence, experience; (3) Apostolic or churchly succession, establishing its proper object, continuity.

1. The so-called evangelical Christianity of the protestant tradition has concentrated on preaching and faith, sometimes almost to the point of ignoring liturgy and institutional succession. Those who stress liturgy and tradition have almost never gone to the same extreme in ignoring the claims of preaching and faith. Preaching and faith, they would say, do their work best when given to us in the context of liturgy and tradition. No one of these three strands was ever meant to function alone and apart from the others. On the contrary they were meant to be plied together, so that the thread of continuity might achieve maximum strength. The values of the protestant tradition reach their highest point of power and efficiency when they are retained within the context of Catholic institutions. Artificially isolated, as in so much of the religious history which has developed out of the Reformation, they assert themselves too stridently and perhaps protest too much. Nevertheless, these values are genuine values from any point of view. The Christian Community proclaims its gospel and the proclamation evokes a vivid faith in the continued presence of Christ in the minds of those who hear. 'He that hath ears to hear let him hear.' The danger of this very one-sided evangelical Christianity is that it relies too much on powerful mental reactions in the minds of those to whom the gospel is proclaimed, so that being a Christian becomes a state of mind rather than taking a certain stand with the Christian community in

the midst of history. Certainly Luther and the great giants of the Reformation never meant by justification by faith merely that the intensity of a man's subjective faith justifies him. Yet, in fact, a doctrine not unlike this became the most striking characteristic of the so-called evangelical Christianity.

The trouble of relying on faith alone is that faith, Christian faith at all events, was never meant to function alone. Rather it was meant to be the subjective accompaniment or counterpart of the objective historic circumstance of being in the Church. Paraphrasing freely, we may say that 'It is not good for faith to be alone.' Faith needs what it responds to, requites what it cohabits with, is always a subjectivity located side by side with an objectivity, like any sane subjectivity. The principle of 'faith alone' misapprehends the nature of faith. For faith is always that in my private mind which keeps me there where I am in the public world of history. Because of faith I stand here in the midst of the Church, praising the Lord, not only secretly, but in the great congregation.

Thus we can indeed re-echo the Christianity of the protestant evangelical tradition in assigning the highest possible value to interior faith, but we cannot for this reason speak of *faith alone*. Faith is an interior reality which has external stimuli, accompaniments and consequences. Nothing can compensate for its absence, but other things must be present also if we are to have it in its integrity.

2. The role of liturgy in the Church is to re-immerse men in the biblical experience considered as a contemporary experience. In the Baptismal and Eucharistic liturgies the Christian stands side by side with other Christians belonging to very different centuries and cultures. Liturgy is the catholic or universal element in Christian experience. Gathered before the altar or the font out of every people and tongue, out of every age and

generation, out of every culture and civilization, we are one. These liturgical experiences are the biblical experiences, experiences of Incarnation and redemption, of creation and miracle, of sanctification and recreation, of supernatural rebirth and death-defying destiny. It is this liturgical experience which makes it possible for Christians to read and enter into the scripture. Without the liturgy scripture must inevitably be received and interpreted from the standpoint of some post-scriptural and non-scriptural frame of mind, but within the liturgy it is received and interpreted from its own standpoint, from the standpoint of the kind of experience to which it was given and to which it testifies. Liturgy is, of course, in no sense independent of faith, and is, indeed, of very little value without faith, but it nevertheless contributes enormously to faith, giving it a habitat and a home, a substance and an objectivity which, without liturgy, faith can hardly possess.

3. Apostolic succession is the mode through which the living Church on earth affirms its visible continuity, its substantial and historical identity with the Church of the ages, the Church of the very earliest times. Christian faith is not the kind of faith that takes note only of the invisibilities and spiritualities ingredient into our existence. It is not a cult of the interior life which relegates the exterior into a kind of outer darkness. God, according to the Nicene Creed, is the creator of all things both visible and invisible. We have already touched upon one aspect or application of this doctrine in insisting upon that usage of the word history which we have called history B. Those events which are visible to the historian and those events which are invisible to him constitute in their objective actuality one single historical succession of events. This, however, is but one aspect of a more general doctrine according to which in actuality the invisible world and the visible world constitute not two worlds but one.

Always the visible has invisible depths, and sometimes at least the invisible has a visible surface. The distinction between the visible and invisible is not ultimate, with the consequence that the social life of the Christian Church consists sometimes of visibilities and sometimes of invisibilities. For the most part the continuity of a church is a visible continuity, manifesting itself in tactual organic succession from generation to generation, and yet at each climatic moment in the succession, at the consecration of each new bishop, we interpret the occasion not merely as one moment in the succession, not merely horizontally, but also vertically as an act of divine initiative, in which God gives to his Church a ministry of the prophetic word and the substantial sacraments which his Church could not, dare not, even pretend to give itself. The Christian Church cannot be an arrogant, Pelagian Church, which by its own act provides itself with its own succession and its own continuity. The life and survival of the Christian Church comes to it from God alone, for the Church is that area or dimension of human experience in which the Christ of centuries ago is known and recognized as the active, persistently relevant Lord of history.

Faith, Liturgy and Apostolic succession can thus be set side by side as the means in and through which the Christ persistently reaffirms himself as always contemporary, as the manifestation in history of that which transcends all history. Of course, as I have already said, these modes of communication might well be ineffective were it not for the tremendous and energetic validity of the truth which they communicate. Yet human faith, which seems at first sight something which men subjectively experience, and Catholic liturgy, which would appear to be an activity in which God and men combine, and apostolic succession, which looks more like a series of divine initiatives, belong together and must be set side by side as composing the three stranded rope by means of which this saving Christian consciousness descends from generation to generation. Certainly these three belong together, and with equal certainty they ought never to be opposed to or estranged from each other. As I have already said, the proper context of the protestant values is the Catholic Church, where Faith, Liturgy and Apostolic succession collaborate to secure this invincible consciousness of the Christ's victorious transcendence of history.

So interpreted, the difference between being in history and being in eternity is not so great as it often seems. Interpreted eschatologically—and the Church here in history must always be interpreted eschatologically—the Church as we know it always appears as a community of experience located on the very edge of eternity, knowing that that eternity is the Kingdom of Christ. For us in Christianity the tribulations of each present time create a patience which is willing to wait until the end of the story to make the substance of its meaning clear, and in turn the patience makes possible a new way of experiencing history, not as a collection of episodes, but as a movement in a certain divine direction, so that the experience in its turn nurtures and nourishes a hope, the saving hope that the Kingdom of God is indeed already prevailing and will at last prevail. There are, no doubt, many reasons for believing that this is not so, but, it might be suggested, there are no reasons at all for believing that anything else is so. Here as elsewhere in Christianity we may echo the cry of Newman, 'Ten thousand difficulties don't make one doubt.' The only alternative to this light is darkness. The only alternative to this rational faith is one of the various feasts of unreason which vast numbers of our contemporaries are busily celebrating in every quarter of our cultural milieu.

CHAPTER 8

THE WORD OF GOD—TO-DAY

IN this book we have in effect rejected the conventional
philosophy of history, the speculative patterns that we
find in such writers as Vico, Hegel, Marx, Spengler, and
even in certain aspects of Toynbee. Such philosophies of
history attempt to trace some universal process of historical
development concerning which historians are perhaps
rightly sceptical. The trouble with this kind of philosophy
of history, indeed, is not so much an obvious dialectical
or metaphysical ineptitude as its almost total failure to
convince working historians. Such a defect is not without
its significance for the philosopher. Of course, we can find
the same kind of trouble elsewhere. Thus there are many
philosophies of science which have very little to do with
what the working, researching scientist is actually engaged
upon, and most of the so-called 'philosophies of religion'
leave the genuinely religious, worshipping man cold and
unimpressed. Clearly the philosophy which attempts to
interpret a phase of human experience should be one that
those actually engaged in scrutinizing the empirical data
scientifically will welcome because it assists them to understand themselves and their task. The failure of the
conventional forms of the philosophy of history to attract
and interest historians is really a sign and symptom of
profoundly philosophical shortcomings.

In this book we have substituted for the idea of a fixed,
regularly recurrent pattern of history an alternative
conception, drawn perhaps from our own interpretation
of Toynbee rather than from Toynbee's interpretation of
himself, of persistent historical themes, so that the philosophy of history, while powerless either to predict the

future or to formulate laws which are supposed to have governed the past, does make possible an understanding of what is at stake in history, an awareness of what the historical drama is about. We have also insisted that the proper theme of the philosophy of history is the examination of the methodology which the historians use, an epistemological analysis of the forms and validity of historical knowledge and, above all, an ontological interpretation of the place and significance of historical events in what we may call the scale of being or reality.

Rightly and inevitably we have laid especial stress on the last of these three philosophical themes. The kind of transitory actuality with which historical events confront us, and, indeed, more generally all temporal events whatsoever, whether historical or not, is indeed a form, one form but not the only form, of reality. Behind this approach to the particular problem of the philosophy of history there lies, in the mind of the author, a general philosophical point of view which might perhaps be described as realistic Platonism, or, even better, total realism. It may be convenient at this point briefly to summarize this general philosophy, even though this is certainly not the place in which to defend it.

According to what I would call realistic Platonism or total realism, things or events located in space-time *exist* for perception; the ideas, scientific or philosophical, in terms of which things and events can be shown to be after all intelligible as well as merely factual *subsist* for thought; God *supersists* for piety and faith. I say that God supersists because it would seem to me obvious that he does not subsist like a platonic universal, nor does he exist like some particular percept. Supersistence combines certain characteristics of subsistence, i.e. universality and comprehensibility, with certain characteristics of existence, i.e. vivid immediacy and concreteness, yet God is neither an idea nor a thing. In the last resort all we can say of

216

such an ultimate singular is that he is himself. God is just God, or Absolute Existence. This is patently obvious to all of us, though some may perversely conceal their knowledge and consciousness of the divine supersistence by labelling God with some other more ambiguous name, like nature, creative evolution, or the dialectic of history.

Nevertheless, we all acknowledge in one way or another some element of finality and ultimacy in reality which shapes our ends rough hew them how we may. There is only one absolute argument for the existence of God, the so-called ontological argument in its many and varied forms. The ground of all possibilities cannot be a mere possibility, just as the class of all classes cannot be merely a member of itself. This would seem to me to be the one absolutely decisive argument in all philosophy, and the many attempts to refute it are all of them based upon a perverse failure to understand it. The question which the ontological argument has raised, ever since St. Anselm formulated the first clear and explicit version of it, is whether whatever it is the necessity of which the argument demonstrates, is to be identified with the God who is worshipped and adored in biblical religion. Such an identification from the point of view of religious faith and theology would seem to me absolutely inevitable, but I can see that there might be purely philosophical grounds for a reluctance to assert it. Unfortunately this is not the place in which to consider and analyse this particular question.

For those who do make this identification, however, an interesting and important implication arises. Faith and piety are, indeed, forms of cognition which are related to subsistent concepts very much as in the Platonic scheme the subsistent concepts are related to the world of percepts. As the concepts to some extent unify and render intelligible the otherwise chaotic and infinitely pluralistic world of percepts, so the acknowledgement of the divine super-sistence unifies and renders intelligible the still mildly chaotic and pluralistic realm of concepts. For when we acknowledge the divine supersistence we assert the reality of an actuality behind even the world of concepts which has some analogy with the actuality of the immediate existences with which we find ourselves environed in the world of nature and history. Mere Platonism, at all events in the later Platonic tradition, exalted the compre-hensibility of concepts over the world of actual things and events a little too crudely. Ultimate reality as we have said, is more than a mere idea; it is actuality also. Hence the term *supersistence* befits its character far better than either *existence* or *subsistence*.

From this point of view the task of philosophy is clear, although at the same time it must necessarily be an exacting and complex one. Any viable system of philo-sophy must be at the same time a philosophy of nature, a philosophy of history, a philosophy of existence and a philosophy of religion and yet remain one comprehensible system of philosophy. Thus a philosophy of nature and natural science, like naturalism, which may be fairly plausible considered simply as a philosophy of nature and natural science, nevertheless fails lamentably because it is a weak philosophy of history, a feeble philosophy of existence and a very poor, uninsightful philosophy of religion. The same thing, *mutatis mutandis*, might be said of any conventional philosophy of history, like Marxism, or almost any form of fashionable existentialism, and of most of the merely religious philosophies of religion. However plausible each may sound in its own chosen field, its gross inadequacy in the other fields betrays its weakness. The true philosopher is never content to be the philo-sopher merely of this or that. His concern is with the interpretation of reality, with everything, and the proper context of the philosophy of this or that is the philosophy of all. Unfortunately in making some particular application of philosophy this is not always sufficiently apparent, and that is why, even in a short book devoted to the philosophy of history, I take this opportunity of indicating in this brief and bare summary the outlines of the total philosophy of which this particular philosophy of history is an integral part, in which, in fact, it takes the form of one brief chapter or digression.

In the terminology indicated in this brief sketch of a total philosophical point of view, history is the realm in which existence approaches most closely to supersistence. That is why the beings involved in the course of history demand, as a necessary part of the philosophical interpretation of their existence, not only a philosophy of history but also an existentialism, for the being of the participants in the drama of history is a personal being which the categories of the philosophy of history cannot entirely comprehend. They are in time, in existence, but they are for eternity, for supersistence. That is why each of them is a philosophical theme in himself. However great the ineptitudes of the existentialists, however extensive the areas of philosophical inquiry which they fail to recognize, this truth at least they have perceived: Man himself, each man, is a philosophical theme.

In understanding and interpreting finite human philosophy it is always necessary to remember that the failure to see something or other is the inevitable by-product of the intense concentration with which we look at something else. This accounts for the characteristic blindness not only of the existentialists but also of the logical philosophers and linguistic analysts of our time. They are looking at something which is really there to be looked at, and really ought to be looked at, but with such concentration and devotion of intellect, admirable in itself, that they are able to perceive nothing else. Always our blindness occurs just beyond the periphery of our vision; or, as someone remarked to me a little time ago after barely escaping what might have been a rather nasty motor accident, 'What a pity that none of us are born with eyes in the back of our heads.' It is indeed unfortunate, but this is the kind of defect which we must learn to endure and live with, and sometimes to take into account before we judge others too harshly.

But there is another characteristic of the traditional philosophy of history in which it very closely resembles theology and which demands our sympathy and approval. It has always been the aim of philosophy of history to serve mankind, to assist men to conduct the course of historical existence more successfully in the future than in the past, by helping them to comprehend more precisely what they are doing, what is at stake in the historical drama. The underlying purpose of the philosophical understanding of history is to make historical action more intelligent. No doubt in this desire to serve mankind philosophy of history is close also to many aspects of sociology, but closest of all to theology, which has always been concerned above everything else with the true end and aim of human existence, identified for theology with the mind, the will, the heart, the creative purpose of its Author. 'Know thyself.' 'Live as befits thy nature.' Christianity has always had this at least in common with Socrates. Even so, philosophy at its best is concerned not with truth only, but also with a ministry of self-understanding to mankind. There is nothing schizophrenic about this, for such self-understanding can only be attained in the light of the truth, and the truth conversely cannot but conduce towards self-understanding.

It would seem obvious that this element shared by philosophy of history and theology in common must necessarily be even more strongly emphasized when we are concerned with Christian or theological philosophy of history. We have a right to expect and demand that out of such a discipline there should emerge some strengthening word of guidance for us to-day, surrounded as we are by the problems and perplexities of our time. Christian philosophy of history must be prophetic in the biblical sense, an understanding of the temporal in the light of the eternal, a human cognition of the historical which approximates towards the divine understanding of it, which issues in the recognition and proclamation of the divine judgement upon it. The supreme question in this and every time is still the question which the harassed King Zedekiah put to Jeremiah, 'Is there any word from the Lord?' That is why I wish to conclude this book with some consideration of the contemporary proclamation of the Christian message and interpretation: What is the Word of the Lord for to-day?

'How shall we sing the Lord's song in a strange land?'[1] This fallen world has always and at all times been a strange and not very suitable place in which to be religious. However, it is the only place we have and so religious men have been compelled all down the ages to do the best they can in and with it. There have, however, been 'no ages of faith.' 'How shall we sing the Lord's song in a strange land?' has always, at all times and in all places, been a very relevant and pertinent inquiry. The difficulties and problems confronting religious faith have differed greatly, but difficulties and problems of some sort there have always been. The tendency of religious men, however, has always been to suppose in every age that nobody before ever had it so bad, to dream of some golden age in the past in which their particular, contemporary problem had not arisen, quite forgetting that one problem only flies out of the window as another enters by the door. The task confronting the Christian Church, for example, has always and in every age of its history been insuperably difficult. Always in history genuine faith and

[1] Psalm 137. 3.

religious understanding has been at the same time absolutely necessary and quite impossible. Nevertheless, to each age of history its own peculiar difficulties, its own pressing perplexities, and to this general rule our time presents no exception. The peculiar problem of our own day is the widespread death of hope, a prevalent feeling that the end of all things is indeed at hand, unrelieved by any faith that this at the same time means that the Kingdom of God is near.

In our world this phenomenon is very largely due to the general decay of the belief in progress. This particular species of historical optimism first arose and became prevalent in the eighteenth century, as an offshoot and consequence of the so-called *aufklarung* of that time. We have already diagnosed it as a transferring of the attributes of sacred history to secular history, a kind of inverted Augustinianism, related to St. Augustine rather as Marx was related to Hegel, who, it is said, he 'stood on his head.' The City of Man was misperceived as the City of God, and usurped its celestial trappings. Small wonder that in the nineteenth century, in Feuerbach and Compte, for example, man himself was invested with the garments of divinity, for, in the City of Man, man is god and not God. The result of these developments was a period in which even people who went to Church on Sundays and sang hymns really lived and were sustained by this optimistic and progressive secular faith. Orthodox Christianity, because of its belief in original sin and the inherent fallenness of the human situation, was even set aside, not only by unbelievers but also by self-consciously modern, liberal-minded Christians, as too pessimistic to sustain the creative wave and surge of modern culture. To such people the world appeared to be getting steadily better, outgrowing its barbarous past, moving by its own inherent momentum towards a condition which had many of the characteristics of the Kingdom of God, even though conceivably this kingdom might, in fact, be a republic in which there was no king. By a strange contrast orthodox Christianity is now set aside, by many existentialists and philosophers of the absurd, for example, as, altogether too crassly optimistic, as an opiate concealing from the people the true rigors and horrors of their tragic situation. We have moved from the world which entertained the wrong hopes, and trusted too lavishly in gods that could not aid them, to a world which more and more refuses to entertain any hope at all. It was altogether too simple to believe that the dying away of the popular faith in progress would throw men back upon a renewed faith in divine providence. There was always an alternative. Beyond hope in God, there lay hope in hope, but beyond hope in hope there lies despair.

The eighteenth-century faith in progress was strongly reinforced in the nineteenth century by a rather ill-considered progressivist interpretation of the doctrine of evolution. Actually, of course, there was very little reason to suppose that the goal of physical evolution was identical with the goal of social progress, but generally the course of historical events, which, as it was supposed, is correctly interpreted by the doctrine of progress, was treated as a mere continuation of physical and biological evolution on the human level. If evolution has contrived to bring the universe to the point at which man emerges, it was assumed, the same forces may likewise contrive to bring man to the point at which the ultimate Kingdom of God or Man likewise emerges. The result was that brand of progressive cosmic optimism which we call progress today, the off-spring of both eighteenth-century philosophical rationalism and nineteenth-century scientific romanticism.

The objections to any such doctrine were always strong. There is, indeed, something almost immoral about it. It certainly implies that the human race is something of incomparably higher value and worth than the human person. Evolutionistic progressivism thought itself moral merely because it inculcated unselfishness. We must strive to-day in order that our remote descendants may to-morrow enter into the kingdom. We must labour that they may enjoy the fruits of our labours. The happiness of the future must be based upon a callous exploitation of the creative energies of the past and the present. The nature of things is such that we are used merely as a means to the future. There may, indeed, be jam to-morrow, but quite certainly there will never be jam to-day. Thus for the truly religious and ethical cult of the passing moment there is substituted the cult of some remote and unimaginable dawn. Of course, it is possible for men to enter into such a faith sincerely, and with a genuine willingness to sacrifice themselves for the sake of the future, but it is also true that such a faith can be callously and cynically abused by the leaders of the people, as to an astounding degree by many of the communists. 'Jam to-morrow but never jam to-day' is an apt slogan for the peddler of 'pi in the future.'

This may be contrasted with the dictum of St. Thomas Aquinas: 'Personality is the most perfect thing in the whole creation,'[1] or that of Immanuel Kant: 'Act always so as to treat thy brother as an end and never as a means to an end.'[2] For progressivism the person is too brief an actuality for us to concern ourselves too much about him. Indeed, he ought not to be too much concerned with himself. It is the race that endures and survives, the race that really matters. Thus there is a genuine link between the nineteenth-century progressivism and the twentieth-century emergence of the totalitarian state, with its characteristic abuse and exploitation of the individual person. After all, if he does not really matter in philosophy, why should we be too concerned about his welfare

[1] *Summa Theologica*, I, 29, 3, c.   [2] *Metaphysics of Morals*. Section II.

and destiny in actual history? The trouble with progressivism, particularly when interpreted in terms of evolution, is that it interprets the realm of persons in too exclusively biological a category. Men are merely complicated animals, and the interpretation of personality as an entirely new order of value and significance is just a religious mistake.

Yet before the Christian thinker sets the doctrine of progress aside, as not merely a gross and even perhaps somewhat ridiculous philosophical error, the underlying ethics of which are not merely dubious in theory but probably brutal in practice, there is perhaps from his own point of view something which ought to be said on the other side. After all, the original condition of man, whether we conceive it with the help of the ethnological sciences or imagine it with the aid of the opening chapters of Genesis, was certainly not the Kingdom of God. Even if there had been no fall and no sin, and human existence and history of a paradisal and non-epic character, there would still have been some process of continuous and cumulative development before the final Kingdom of God became a possibility. This might even have included the Incarnation, although certainly not the Cross. Duns Scotus and certain other great Christian theologians have held—although possibly this is a minority view—that even though there had been no sin and no fall and man had needed no redemption the Incarnation would nevertheless have taken place, for the Incarnation is an essential element in the whole process of creation. In other words, although the gospel story would have been very different, there would still have been a gospel story. All this, of course, is very speculative. All we know for certain is that there was sin and there was a redemptive Incarnation. Whether even without sin there would have been a kind of revelatory Incarnation, which at the same time rendered complete the whole scheme and pattern of evolution, we cannot be sure. At best the view associated with Duns Scotus must remain a mere pious opinion.

Nevertheless, this pious opinion does make possible a Christian insight about the doctrine of progress which might otherwise never occur to us. Something at all events very like what we mean by progress might have been characteristic of the historical process if there had been no sin and no fall. In that case men might have moved through a peaceful and creative, and no doubt rather shorter, historical process from their humble beginnings to the fullness of their development in the flowering Kingdom of God. Even in history as it is we can trace dim vestiges of this original progressive pattern over considerable periods of time, so that fallen history is still sufficiently progressive and cumulative in appearance to produce in certain relatively peaceful and creative periods the illusion that the doctrine of progress may perhaps be true. It is to these vestiges of the original pattern that progressivists persistently draw attention. Thus there are periods in which the sciences and technologies develop rapidly both in comprehensiveness and effectiveness. It is even possible to trace a genuine degree of religious development in the world. We may cite as an analogy the view, the majority view in Christendom, that the sin and fall of man did not entirely obliterate the image of God in man. Even in the world and history as they are we still see in man as he is the vestiges of the original magnificent conception. Again and again the image is thwarted, repressed and caricatured, but it is never altogether lost to sight. Thus progress is what would have happened without sin and the fall, and the vestiges of it are sufficient to persuade some thinkers that despite sin and the fall progress is what is happening now. Of course, this progress that might have been but is not would have been a very different kind of progress from anything which the conventional progressivists conceive or imagine, but it would certainly have been something even more deserving of the name than what, even according to the progressivists, has actually occurred.

Thus the Christian, in decisively rejecting the doctrine of progress, must at least allow it this partial validity. If there had been no sin and no fall there would not have been that distinction between sacred history and secular history on which the whole Augustinian doctrine of providence and history hinges. In fact, according to the Christian view, the gracious providence of God, which first made itself manifest in the activity of creation, once it had most graciously permitted itself to be frustrated on that level, expresses its sovereignty by reasserting itself as redemption, so that now it is the forces of redemption which manifest that progressive character which originally and in principle belong to all history whether sacred or secular.

The trouble about progress, once it has been transferred from sacred history to secular history, is its liability to a terrible disillusion. In the twentieth century we have been the horrified witnesses of a re-emergence of barbarism, a sophisticated barbarism which has made the fullest use of the resources placed at its disposal by our boasted science and technics, in order to be the more effective in the pursuit of its lethal purposes. We destroy this technologically-equipped barbarism in one form only to see it apparently risen from the dead in some other guise. In the form of Germanic nationalism it has menaced the world twice in a single generation. Once powerful western countries like France and Britain have squandered vast resources of blood and treasure, and a decade of civilized energy which might otherwise have been used for more creative purposes, in a brave and noble effort to overcome the teutonic menace. They were left in consequence well-nigh bankrupt and ruined. To have played the part which they have played is an honourable and epic thing, but its cost to them has been incalculable and may yet prove fatal. But now, after all this has been endured, the same hideous evil, more powerful and destructive than ever, may possibly confront us in Soviet Communism. Has the struggle perhaps to be endured all over again, at a cost more ruinous and with consequences more dire and destructive than ever before?

The now triumphant development of our boasted sciences and our valued technology places in human hands lethal weapons with an effectiveness beyond the wildest and most ambitious dreams of all previous barbarians and aggressors. Apparently that which our optimistic secular progressivists most of all counted and relied upon has risen up to betray their ideals. We look backward into the immediate past and all, or almost all, is darkness—not the darkness of ignorance but the darkness of knowledge, not the darkness in which there is no knowledge, but rather a darkness that is known. We look forward into the impending future and again all is darkness—not the darkness of ignorance but the darkness of fear, fear of a fatality more terrible than anything that went before. All this modern man experiences without the biblical faith which would bid him look up when he sees these things come to pass, for behold, his redemption draweth nigh. For our secular progressivism, which is after all a kind of secularized biblicism, has for vast numbers of people destroyed the faith that might have enabled them to survive these terrible disillusions.

The consequence is a widespread despair. If life does not possess the meaning and purpose which progressivism assigned to it, if history is not a process which the doctrine of progress correctly analyses and interprets, then there is no meaning, and life is ultimately and inherently absurd. The doctrine of life as absurd, now so prevalent and influential among intellectuals and dreamers all over our civilization, cannot be fully discussed in the present context. Indeed, it is a doctrine which deserves a book all to itself. According to this doctrine life has no meaning inherent in itself which it sets before us. If life is to have any meaning at all it must be the meaning which we give to it, foisting an alien and external meaning upon the chaotic and meaningless, as the gods of pagan mythology once imposed the semblance of cosmic order upon a reluctant and recalcitrant chaos. We must not deceive ourselves; if life has no meaning of its own it is useless for us even to pretend to impose upon it some private human meaning to which it must inevitably prove altogether intractable. Reality is pitiless and blind. It is indifferent to all values and all purposes whatsoever. The most we can ask and hope for is that we may not be deceived—that we may have the courage to face the realities of a bleak and comfortless situation and with our last breath curse and repudiate it before it bears down upon us and destroys us.

For such a doctrine it is from chaos that we come and to chaos that we must return. Indeed, even in the brief interval between these two events, we are ourselves but ridiculous offshoots of chaos, the spawn of the absurd, as absurd as all our fathers were. The meaning we endeavour to give to life is never, alas, life's meaning, and we define and live by that meaning, whatever it is, ultimately in vain. Hope of any kind is impossible without illusion, and what awakened man worthy of truth would even ask to be deceived?

For most people all this is bleak and uninviting doctrine, but we cannot for that reason deny that it might nevertheless be the truth. It is, after all, related to elements in classical philosophy, even in classical Christianity. For both of these traditions the world in its sheer brute givenness is not rational. These contemporary pessimists, so much more creative in the literary sense than almost any previous generation of philosophers, so that we find their views in exceedingly readable plays and novels rather than in weighty philosophical tomes, speak of cosmic absurdity where their predecessors spoke of the contingency of the world. From the point of view of the Christian philosopher they seem to analyse created being, including their own, and, finding that it lacks the absoluteness and *aseity* of God, they therefore conclude that it cannot really be anything at all. They forget the glory of what contingent being is in a horrified acknowledgement of what it is not and cannot be. The world is not God and therefore it is ultimately nothing. The absurd in contemporary philosophy is thus the counterpart of the contingent in traditional philosophy, but whereas the acknowledgement of the contingency led the traditional-philosopher to God, the modern trick of calling the contingent the absurd leads the contemporary philosopher to nihilism. 'Unless there is no God,' said Nietzsche, 'man cannot become God.' The modern philosopher of the absurd has established to his own satisfaction that there is indeed no God, or at least, as he thinks, succeeded in demonstrating the absence of God from the human scene, but still he finds that man cannot become God. 'Even if there is no God,' he might reply to Nietzsche, 'man cannot become God.' The alternative to God is not the divination of superman; the alternative to God is the absurd.

But it is not merely that something corresponding to what the modern philosopher calls the absurd, though otherwise and very differently conceived and defined, is present in traditional Christian philosophy. That philosophy also presses upon us another and even more incisive question. From what point of view is the absurd recognized and known to be what it is? If, indeed, all were absurd we could not even perceive and define the absurdity of the absurd. The absurd is always absurd from a rational point of view. If all is, indeed, absurd, the knowledge of the absurd would be impossible. Behind this existentialist pessimism we can discern the outlines of the man who is to the Greeks a rational animal, to the Christian a child of God, the man who knows the absurd when he sees it, who carries about within himself the criteria that enable him to look at life and cry, 'Ridiculous!'

There is, indeed, a Christian doctrine of the absurd. For Christian thought sin is the absurd, that groundless and totally unrevealing element in life which conceals the true character of actuality. That is why in Christianity, as we have seen, evil is not truly and ultimately real. It has tragic historical actuality but no metaphysical substance. So to speak, it is here but not there. Behind its hideous mask there lurks—nothing. But, here again, we see clearly that the absurd is, and can only be recognized as, absurd for and by a rational mind and in a rational system.

Nevertheless, despite this basic absurdity of the philosophy of the absurd, an interior self-contradiction which is fatal to its philosophical claims, we must all agree that it does crystallize and express a widespread mood which is present in the minds of many who would be neither able nor willing to provide such explicit formulations and assents. This radical pessimism is the sophisticated rationalization of the much more widespread death of hope. It is the rationalization of an irrational mood.

This, then, is the bleak world which constitutes the very strange land in which the contemporary Christian is called upon to sing the Lord's song. Once, as we have seen, he was condemned for being too gloomily pessimistic; now he is taken to task for his crass optimism, so inferior both intellectually and morally, we are told, to the courageous outlook of the total pessimist who is unafraid to face the gloomy emptiness of existence. In whatever way the spirit of the age chooses to make the comparison, we Christians always come off worst. We have been accused of so many things; it is at least comforting to know that we cannot possibly be guilty of them all.

In this desperate situation we Christians must beware of two very plausible and persuasive temptations. First of all, we must refrain from any vulgar rejoicing over the prevalent death of hope. The progressivist hope may have been a snare and a delusion, misconceived and ill-defined, but at least it was a hope, and it did tend towards the creation and the maintenance of a genuine morale. The man who has lost it and gained nothing else is poorer, not richer, than before. Such a hope could even sustain a kind of ethic which, despite all its obsession with the secular, nevertheless manifested something of that supernatural quality which any genuine ethic must possess. At least it enabled some men, many men, indeed, most of the men part of the time and some of the men most of the time, to transcend the promptings of their own incarnate condition and the lure of their own interests. It was at least a faith which could make men disinterested and provoke in them a degree of integrity as they functioned in their historical roles. But those who clung to this hope departed too easily from the faith that gave it life. To-day in some writers little seems to be left except the service of our interests and the indulgence of our appetites. To-morrow we die, let us at least eat and drink, even though we cannot hope to be merry. One writer reminds us that even if we surrender to Communist dictatorship, as twenty years ago we refused to surrender to the menace of its twin brother Nazism, we shall still be able to eat and drink and sleep with women.

> Thus repulsed, our final hope
> Is flat despair: we must exasperate
> The almighty victor to spend all his rage
> And that must end us; that must be our cure—
> To be no more. Sad cure! For who would lose,

232

Though full of pain, this intellectual being,
Those thoughts that wander through eternity,
To perish rather, swallowed up and lost
In the wide womb of uncreated night,
Devoid of sense and motion? . . .

Wherefore cease we then?
Say they who counsel war; we are decreed,
Reserved, and destined to eternal woe;
Whatever doing, what can we suffer more,
What can we suffer worse? Is this, then, worst—
Thus sitting, thus consulting, thus in arms?[1]

This we may recollect is the counsel of Belial; to seek some kind of contemptuous toleration from the complacent conqueror, who will hardly think such vestiges of our way of our life as we are able to retain worthy of his majestic interference. In any case, of course, to do this rather than that will be as absurd and meaningless as to do that rather than this. The time has gone by for the summons to a doomed crusade. The death of hope means the total eclipse of morale, the extinction of the natural energies following thus closely and inevitably upon the loss of the supernatural faith. Such is certainly not a spectacle over which the Christian can rejoice.

The Christian must beware also of the mistake of merely saying 'I told you so.' No doubt there were Christians who warned mankind in vain about the time when the progressivist fallacy first arose but, to be perfectly honest, we must admit that large numbers of Christians both then and since have done nothing of the kind. But, in any case, to remark that we bore our witness faithfully once is irritatingly beside the point when what we have to do is to bear our witness faithfully now. What confronts us now is not the error of the previous errors but the consequence

[1] Milton, *Paradise Lost*. Book II.

of those errors, and that is a very different and more terrible thing.

On the other hand, the Christian, if he is true to himself, cannot altogether share the chronic obsession of so many of his contemporaries with mere survival. The hope that mankind may prove either too intelligent or too righteous to precipitate nuclear conflict is perhaps a thin and un-convincing one. The historical omens are emphatically not propitious. Again and again in the past men have been guilty of the most stupid and destructive follies. Repeatedly and wantonly they have committed the most catastrophic crimes. We cannot with any confidence assume that they will not do again the kind of thing which they have done so often in the past. There are those who think that such a fatality would end the life and history of man upon this planet. But, after all, the idea of a cata-strophic conclusion to human life and history is itself a biblical notion. For the Christian it would mean that biblical passages which he had previously been prone to interpret as flights of vivid poetic imagery must be taken rather more literally than generations of liberal-minded Christians have supposed. Biblical faith would still insist, however, that the end of the world is but the obverse of the beginning of the Kingdom of God, so that even here Christian hope could look up and behold our redemption drawing nigh. Other observers believe that a nuclear holocaust would decimate rather than destroy the human race, and that the casualty would be not so much mankind itself as our modern, in substance primarily western, type of civilization. The scattered handful of survivors would be in for a kind of new agrarian dark ages, a period lasting for perhaps several centuries in which men would eke out a precarious existence in the pre ent, jealously treasuring small surviving scraps of their past, and almost unconsciously preparing themselves for some new re-emergence of human greatness in the future.

But we must insist that the historic dark ages were not altogether a bad thing. They had their own kind of goodness, not merely the goodness of being a season of seedtime and preparation for the great medieval and modern renaissances, but also an intrinsic goodness of their own in and for themselves. To justify and vindicate a period of history merely in terms of what it led to centuries later is to use the progressivist language of jam to-morrow but never jam to-day, to acquiesce in the basically immoral idea that one generation in history can be written off as a mere means to another. On the contrary, every age has its own value, its own immediacy of access to God. The dark ages were no more an unambiguously bad thing than the present age is an unambiguously good one. If historical and human time were to continue through thousands of years in peaceful progress up to its theoretic limit, whatever that may be, something very strange, indeed, almost miraculous, would have occurred, entirely out of place in the drama of human history. It would seem to be obvious that if man and history continue so long there must inevitably be another dark age at some time or other. There is no way of immunizing fallen man, with his chronic sin and selfishness, against catastrophe. If the destruction of our civilization does not occur at this time, as a consequence of our mishandling of this particular crisis, then it will almost certainly occur at some other time. Here, indeed, we have no continuing city and no abiding stay.

In other words, it behoves us at the present time to be mentally and spiritually prepared for either the end of *the* world or at least the end of *our* world. This means that we must have in our minds the possibility of interpreting either of these events in such a way—that is prophetically, in terms of the judgement of God—as will ensure the survival and fulfilment of hope. After all, the Christian hope is essentially the hope that God will establish the

Kingdom. Christian faith is trust in God, not trust in man. Christian love is the divine love, not human love. Similarly, Christian hope is the conviction that God will be merciful as well as just, not the hope that man will be wise and righteous. We live in a world in which at any time the worst may happen, but at the same time in a world in which the best will certainly happen because it is God's will, not ours.

In these circumstances the really important thing is not survival but responsiveness to judgement, an acceptance of the sternness of history as just, issuing not necessarily in survival but in a moral and spiritual fitness to survive.

The somewhat ambiguous Darwinian appropriation of the term 'survival of the fittest' has perhaps made it rather difficult to use the phrase in any other context, but certainly, speaking in the tradition of the biblical prophets, we can insist that the chief business of contemporary civilization and culture at this juncture is not so much to ensure survival—for, indeed, survival cannot be ensured—but rather with our worthiness and fitness to survive. As we survey the long record of human history we cannot honestly feel that we could have any adequate grounds for complaint if God were to take the view that the time has come to abandon the great experiment of creation as a failure. Of course, we Christians do not believe that God will, in fact, take that view, but we must admit that we should be hard put to it if we were to attempt to demonstrate that such a decision would be unreasonable and unjust.

Even on the eve of a possible armageddon, in other words, the chief duty of man is precisely what it is at all other times, the duty to establish justice, righteousness, and the love that tolerates and encourages freedom among men, to give culture and civilization intrinsic value and significance before God rather than merely to prolong its physical life. To survive ignobly would be far worse than not to survive at all. Paradoxically this is the conviction which, were it sufficiently authoritative over our lives and binding enough to redirect them, would most of all conduce towards survival. Always the chief business of man is not to guarantee his future but to take his '*Now*,' his immediate present, and align it more perfectly with the will of the God of justice and love. '*Now*' is the moment of the judgement of this world, and '*Now*' is the time that may conceivably be accepted. We are not the lords of the future but the faithless, or faithful, stewards of the present.

At the same time the Christian must do justice to his incarnate condition. Here and now his religious existence is inherently an existence in the world. Like the Christ, the Christian must accept the uttermost rigors inherent in his membership of the human race. He has to practise brotherhood, not merely an eschatological brotherhood in the Kingdom, but the present fact of the brotherhood of all men in this fallen world. The price of being a human being has been inflated enormously during the last generation or so, but it is still a price which we must be prepared to pay gladly. We must not even desire to escape the destiny of mankind, however grim that destiny may be. Of course we cannot in fact even hope to escape that destiny, but we should compromise, perhaps irretrievably, our work and witness among men if we permitted ourselves even to wish to do so. The Christian must accept his tragic involvement in the human situation as something essential to his incarnate vocation. Of course, we may, indeed, must, say to our contemporary brother man, 'We cannot share your illusions. We understand why your hopes withered as you grasped them. We know that they had neither substance nor root. Nevertheless, this at least we can and will joyfully do. We will be with you in all your ordeals, and for the sake of the destiny that is set before us we will suffer with you all that you may be called upon to suffer. If need be we will accompany you even through the valley of the shadow of death.'

Of course, it may very well be replied that we can have no alternative, and in the physical sense at least this is obviously true, but there is a great difference between being compelled to suffer with our friends and neighbours, simply because we are inevitably in their vicinity, and actively willing to suffer with them, knowing that such a compassion is the characteristic way of redemptive love. For we have a last message to those who realize that now the hour of judgement and calamity has come, who recognize in some brief, final illumination that no earthly hope can save them. 'Look up,' we must cry, 'for now, indeed, our redemption draws nigh,' adding, perhaps in the last split second before the bomb falls, 'To-day we shall be together—in paradise.'